THE WAYSIDE GARDENS COLLECTION

The SMALL GARDEN

THE WAYSIDE GARDENS COLLECTION

The SMALL GARDEN

A Practical Guide to Planning & Planting

Julie Toll

John E. Elsley, General Editor for The Wayside Gardens Collection

Sterling Publishing Co., Inc. New York

Library of Congress Cataloguing-in-Publication Data

Toll, Julie.
    The small garden :   a practical guide to planning & planting   /
Julie Toll.
        p.   cm.   —   (The Wayside Gardens collection)
    Includes index.
    ISBN 0-8069-3833-1
    1. Landscape gardening.   I. Title.   II. Series.
SB473.T635   1995
635.9–dc20   95-18313
                                                          CIP

        2 4 6 8 10 9 7 5 3 1

Published 1995 by Sterling Publishing Company, Inc.
        387 Park Avenue South, New York, N.Y. 10016

The Wayside Gardens Collection edition

© 1995 Conran Octopus Limited
The original edition first published
in Great Britain by Conran Octopus Limited
37 Shelton Street, London WC2H 9HN
Text and original planting schemes © 1995 Julie Toll
Design and layout © 1995 Conran Octopus Limited
Distributed in Canada by Sterling Publishing
℅ Canadian Manda Group, One Atlantic Avenue, Suite 105
Toronto, Ontario, Canada M6K 3E7
Printed and bound in Hong Kong
All Rights Reserved

American Project Editor   Hannah Steinmetz
Project Editor   Jane O'Shea
Project Art Editor   Ann Burnham
Editors   Carole McGlynn
                           Caroline Davison
Designer   Lesley Craig
Picture Researcher   Helen Fickling
Production   Clare Blackwell
Illustrators   Lynn Chadwick
                           Vanessa Luff
                           Andrew Farmer
                           Valerie Price

        Sterling ISBN 0-8069-3833-1

FRONT JACKET Alchemilla mollis *with* Geranium
endressii.

BACK JACKET *The length of this garden has been used
to maximum effect by creating different "rooms";
sculptural planting reinforces the composition.*

PAGE 1 *The afternoon sun brightens this secluded
and mysterious outdoor room.*

PAGE 2 *Pots of fuchsias, pelargoniums and* Impatiens
*introduce summer color to this well-structured
garden.*

RIGHT *The bold use of granite cobblestones and
stone walling is softened by the bright green carpet
of* Soleirolia soleirolii, *an alternative to grass which
is effective in a small space.*

CONTENTS

THE JOY OF SMALL GARDENS

If you view a modest garden as an intimate outdoor room which can be shaped to meet individual needs, you will have an idea of the use, versatility and importance of this small space. The outdoor room plays a key part in our modern lives and should not only be attractive all year round but must also be functional and provide maximum enjoyment for its owners by exploiting every nook and cranny. With good design, the small garden can cater to a wide range of activities while remaining a pleasurable oasis in all seasons.

In this charming outdoor room, the paved lower terrace balances and contrasts with the different color and texture of the granite stone paving. Sheltered by a large sun umbrella, it makes a pleasant sitting and dining terrace. This well-proportioned paved garden relies on the foliage and form of the planting to bring interest to it. The bold leaves of the huge Gunnera manicata in a large terra-cotta pot form a dramatic focal point within the garden and contrast with the tall flower spikes of the nearby Acanthus.

Simplicity is the key to good design in a miniature space. This restful composition of silver, green and white flowers and foliage, including hydrangea, arum lily and Convolvulus cneorum, *associates well with the natural colors of brick and terra-cotta pots and the texture of gravel.*

RIGHT *The composition of a garden has to work when it is viewed from upstairs as well as at ground level. Structural plants strengthen this design, while the pastel color scheme, with gray and white, softens the ground pattern created by the paved surfaces. A* Magnolia grandiflora *clothes the house wall with its glossy foliage and scented flowers.*

How big is a small garden?

Small has different meanings for different people. Some may think of a small garden as being somewhat less than a quarter of an acre but this book concentrates on really small spaces, not exceeding 60 ft. by 33 ft. There are many gardens of this size, and smaller, all over the world, in both town and country locations.

One of my design commissions was for a house with a front garden measuring 20 ft. by 10 ft. and a back garden measuring 27 ft. by 18 ft.—little more than the size of a large sitting room. Another way to envisage the size of a small plot is to picture a tennis court (approximately 115 ft. by 56 ft. and realize that at least two of the largest gardens I describe will fit into this space.

There is a tendency to associate small gardens with town houses but many can be found with houses in coastal regions and the cottages of small communities adjacent to open countryside, as well as in newer developments in the suburbs or on the edge of larger communities. A substantial farmhouse may have a very small front garden as the only place in which to sit or grow decorative plants, all the land behind being given over to agriculture or the farmyard. And with many apartments, a green outdoor room has to be created on a roof or balcony.

The challenges and the rewards

There are inevitably certain challenges associated with small gardens which must be met when you plan or redesign your plot. A small garden is often attached to one of the main rooms in the house, putting it constantly on view, while at the same time it may be a regular route through to the house, the shed, the garage or just to hang out the washing. It must be designed and planted to look attractive at all times, while still providing access. Many small plots are enclosed and their boundaries, forming a significant part of the design, could all too easily be overbearing. Careful choice of materials and their integration within the overall garden concept is therefore critical. The proximity of nearby buildings and trees can be a problem in small urban plots, causing particular climatic effects over which the owner has no control; the selection and placing of plants therefore needs special consideration. Restricted space puts pressure on every inch and the surfaces, both hard paving and the soft-landscaping of lawns and beds, must be planned to withstand wear and tear and still look pleasing. Limited access and storage need to be taken into account all the time, in terms of bringing construction materials, compost or plants through the house, storing tools, and disposing of garden trash promptly.

But creating a successful small garden can be great fun and the rewards are many. In practical terms, the end result is more achievable than it is in a garden of several acres, especially if you are doing everything yourself, and there should be less need for compromise in terms of the materials you use—you can consider laying a small patio in mellow-colored natural flagstones whereas for a terrace three times the size you may have to opt for the cheaper, more uniform concrete paving slabs. There is in a small plot a realistic prospect. of completion within a foreseeable time scale and once the garden is created, its upkeep will take less hours than a larger plot, giving you more time to enjoy the fruits of your labors. There is a wealth of materials, plants, furnishings and themes appropriate to the small garden. With good design, it is possible to fit all the features you want into the garden without crowding it and losing its balance, while the use of clever design tricks can make a diminutive space look significantly larger.

All the best ideas would be wasted without thoughtful planting to give the garden its special atmosphere. The plant selection is crucial since the reduced space gives every plant greater prominence and the shape, foliage interest and flower color, as well as the association of each plant with another, will be observed at close quarters. Careful thought must be given to the integration of plants with the garden's structure and features so that the whole will have a unity that gives the garden its charm.

Continuing plant breeding has led to new hybrids and cultivars with a more compact habit of growth and a longer flowering season, giving us a wider range from which to choose. *Skimmia Japonica* 'Rubella and *Euonymus fortunei* 'Harlequin' are two recent introductions well suited to a small space, both being evergreen and compact in their habit. But there is no need to think only in terms of small plants for a small garden. Indeed, a surprisingly wide range of ultimately large plants are candidates for small spaces; it is their suitability to the soil and the microclimate that makes them successful.

There is a current emphasis on plants grown for their scent, another essential element for small gardens where the close confines intensify smells as well as sights and sounds. Provided the garden has a well-thought-out planting plan, there is much scope for the plant enthusiast to experiment and add to the scheme. With my own small garden I constantly find new species that must be tried without upsetting the overall design. But with the removal of odd failures and the expansion of my collection of pots on the patio, there is room for an amazing number of different plants. Do not be put off by a restricted space—simply make it work harder.

Influences from the past

Many of the design ideas used in today's small spaces have been borrowed from historical gardens, both large and small. Indeed, in many ways we have come full circle: it is ironical that today's small private gardens form an integral part of the living unit, much as they did in the days of the early monastic gardens, where the whole building centered on the internal courtyard garden.

There has always been a strong tradition of enclosing gardens within boundaries, creating small private sanctuaries whose function varied according to the local climate and way of life. The first enclosures were strictly utilitarian and comprised thorny hedges or mud walls to keep out animals and thieves. In time they were replaced with walls and more decorative trellis, fences and flowering hedges. Many of the ornate trellis panels used today are based on historical designs and they add a classical touch to numerous small formal gardens.

In the Spanish gardens of the Moorish period, which evolved from the enclosed "paradise gardens" of Persia, it was common to have formal water features such as canals and fountains within walled courtyards, furnishing a shady retreat in the hot Mediterranean climate. One modern interpretation of this, to have water flowing through narrow runnels constructed in brick, and ending in a still pool or fountain pool, provides an appealing focus in a small formal garden. The symmetrically planted trees of the larger Moorish gardens might be replaced by a pair of formally clipped evergreens grown in large containers, symmetrically placed.

Food production was the main theme of Roman country gardens, although a few flowering plants and aromatic herbs were occasionally included among the vegetables. The wealthier town folk often painted a landscape on the wall at the end of their town gardens—an idea used in today's *trompe l'oeil* designs, which often incorporate planting as well. A painted picture will portray a scene and hide an ugly wall.

Medieval gardens were usually square or rectangular, and often enclosed, based on the earlier monastery gardens in which vegetables, medicinal plants and herbs were grown, each in their own small enclosed area. Intricate patterns were sometimes created, with the use of scented herbs, trellis and arbors. A small version of this "knot" garden can be re-created in a sunny courtyard today, using low clipped hedges, scented shrubs, sweet-smelling climbers and evergreen herbs to form the enclosed beds, divided from each other by brick or gravel paths, and guaranteeing perpetual fragrance and year-round interest.

During the Italian and French Renaissance, gardens were much larger and laid out on a grand scale, with terraces, formal planting and formal lawns separated by wide paths. This theatrical "set" was used to display statues, urns and busts as well as water features such as fountains and classical period furniture. Adapting this theme to the scale of a small formal garden, we can create a classical setting in which to display traditional or contemporary artifacts within the confines of a relatively miniature space. The secret is to keep the setting very simple, yet to be bold with the use of large, well-tended plants and sculpture or statuary. Provided it has balance, with the plants and the paved spaces in scale with the objects displayed, the garden of a well-proportioned period town house will take substantial architectural furnishings.

The author, Julie Toll, seen in her garden in early summer.

RIGHT *Classical themes can be adapted to the scale of a small formal garden if the setting is kept simple.*

BELOW *The use of* trompe l'oeil *dates back to Roman times and is used in this garden, in Charleston, South Carolina, to transform a barren wall into a pleasing backdrop. The use of a mirrored arch and trellis fixed against the wall adds interest to the wall, deceiving the eye as well as giving an impression of greater space.*

During the nineteenth century, large gardens were broken down into smaller compartments, each with their own character or theme. Geometric design prevailed and clipped hedges, formal water features and orderly plant displays were common. Any or several of these elements can become a feature of the smaller garden of today.

The introduction of plants from other parts of the world reached a peak during this century and it is partly due to the great nineteenth-century plant explorers that there is for our small spaces such a wide range of species, with an emphasis on plants to soften an urban outlook. Although the first herbaceous borders were generally designed on a large scale, we can still learn much from the plant associations and the strong use of color to help us create our own mixed plantings, more appropriate to smaller spaces.

While history has taught us much of what we know about gardening and introduced us to so many varied styles and influences, we must continue to look forward, not forgetting that we have the ability to create our own innovative style. With any small garden, the main objective is to integrate the utilitarian with the more aesthetic, visual features to create a place of beauty and tranquility to suit our contemporary way of life.

PLANNING YOUR SMALL SPACE

The main objective at the planning stage is to realize the potential of your small garden. Whether you are carrying out only minor alterations to an existing garden, or undertaking the complete transformation of a derelict or brand-new plot, it is important to plan it out on paper. This helps you to focus your thoughts and avoid the piecemeal syndrome where ideas are randomly incorporated, causing the garden to develop without any overall theme or design. In reality, planning can save you money too, ensuring that you reorganize the garden in a logical order, spending as and when funds are available.

This garden has been planned to utilize its length and to create "rooms" for interest en route through it. Trellis above the boundary walls gives privacy without overpowering the narrow space. The sculptural planting reinforces the composition of the garden, while the sundial provides a focal point when viewed from the house or the far end of the garden. The brick steps and walls echo the house material.

Getting to know your garden

A mature yew hedge, although it may not be the first choice for a small-garden boundary, is worth retaining for the privacy it brings and the dramatic evergreen backdrop it gives for other planting, such as the pots of pelargoniums and verbena here. The uneven brick paving, while it has an attractive, natural appearance, would need to be relaid in a surface used for seating or walking on.

Before starting to make a plan, you should get to know your plot intimately so that you can assess its advantages and disadvantages through the seasons. The best way to go about this is to note down your observations about the existing plants and the condition of the soil, as well as the amount and position of sun and shade at different times of day. Make notes over a period of a year or so, in addition to considering how you will use the space, before deciding on the scale of the alterations. You will then know whether you need to start again or can simply improve what you have. Minor alterations to existing planting and surfaces can often successfully transform an unsightly mess into a very acceptable alternative, but you may conclude that you need to embark on a major redesigning project.

Existing planting

If time allows, study the merits of each plant through the different seasons, before you decide what to save and what to discard. Remember that a well-rooted, established plant takes several years to replace, so do not be hasty and remove mature shrubs which could blend into a new design, giving instant height and structure. Trees and hedges, especially deciduous species, take on a different character as the year progresses. A particular challenge in a small garden is meeting the need for privacy and yet achieving a good balance of sun and shade in both winter and summer. A garden overlooked by neighboring windows or surrounded by other backyards might enjoy the privacy afforded by a dense canopy of foliage in midsummer but after fall leaf fall it may become unacceptably bleak and overlooked and remain so throughout the winter. Planting tall evergreens would help to alleviate the winter effect but may overpower the summer scene, making the garden too cool and shady for outdoor living. I would aim for a garden that is private in summer, when it is most used, and as sunny as possible in winter, to warm and dry the soil and to encourage early new spring growth. An existing hedge or a dense planting of shrubs may act as a good sound or wind barrier, so note its effect in winter and summer before deciding whether to remove it.

Remedial pruning can often help to re-establish an ordered look and improve the original design within an old garden; if in doubt, always try this before removing the shrub or tree entirely (see page 94). There is no point in being sentimental and hanging on to a tree that is dying, however, as it will probably blow down in the next gale.

Lawns are often in a poor state, especially if a garden has been untended for some time. A tall, uncut sward may look as though it is beyond repair, but once it is cut down and the long grass raked off, it may well recover. At first the newly cut grass will be yellowy-brown and look almost dead, but within days it should gradually revive, becoming greener and making new growth. Provided the lawn grasses were good quality, with a regime of feeding and regular mowing a lawn can be made acceptable again. After a trial period, you can decide whether to resod, reseed or keep the existing lawn (see page 92). A garden infested with perennial weeds such as ground elder requires immediate attention; severe problems can take up to a year to resolve.

An established pear tree has been incorporated into the lawn in this re-organized garden. Brick steps and a grouping of pots abundantly filled with Argyranthemum frutescens lead the eye to the upper garden.

Surfaces and features

The structural parts of the garden must also be assessed before you decide what to retain and what to replace. It is a false economy to hang on to structural features that will always be, at best, a compromise. You may wish to redesign the garden's layout altogether, budget permitting, if you dislike the present materials and the general layout. If you only use your outdoor room after work, and your existing patio receives sun only up to midday, you will want to relocate it in the corner of the garden that receives evening sun. In a small plot, one needs to be ruthless

and to assess realistically both the potential longevity and the suitability of the existing hard surfaces. Poor-quality, unsuitable and/or unattractive materials that are out of keeping with the surroundings will let down the entire design.

Most well-executed hard landscaping should last for a considerable time but if a surface or structure is damaged you will need to repair or replace it. Cracks in paving joints could be due to an unstable sub-base, which may need to be relaid—lift up a loose paving slab and look critically at what is underneath. Warning bells should ring if you find only a thin layer of sand or a crumbling, shallow concrete sub-base. Cracked paving slabs may have been made from materials that are not frost-hardy and were therefore unsuitable in the first place, so they would have to be replaced. If in doubt, seek professional advice before spending money on repairs to no avail.

Wooden structures have a limited life, especially those that are in constant contact with moisture in the soil. Fence posts will definitely need replacing in time; treated timber will have a life of between 15 and 20 years, whereas untreated timber may last only three to five years. Check for soft spots in the timber, especially where a post goes into the ground; this indicates rot. Look at the joints where fence panels are fixed to the posts—secure them with new wooden pegs or galvanized fixings if they need repair. Always check the soundness of a wooden arbor or gazebo before training new climbing plants up it; rustic timber is very vulnerable to rot. On a wet, windy day the structure will be carrying a lot of weight.

Water features are a prime source of likely problems. Leaks may only become apparent after a period of dry weather, when you notice that the water level has dropped. Fountains and small water-falls, driven by a pump, are notoriously problematic and, if you buy a house in winter when the system is switched off, always check the waterproofing to see if you need to carry out any leak-repairs. At this stage it is also worth investigating the routes of any power or water supplies and checking electrical safety devices, cabling and the soundness of pipes.

Understanding your soil

It is vital to get to know the type of soil you have, and its condition. Is it very friable and of an open structure or has it been compacted by heavy machinery? Is it fairly lifeless, with little evidence of organic matter and therefore very few, if any, worms present? Is it a heavy, cold, wet soil or one with larger particles and more freely drained? Picking up a handful of soil, feeling its texture and observing the growth of plants in it will answer these questions. A healthy root system cannot develop in poor soil conditions and plants growing in lifeless soil will show signs of slow annual growth and be more prone to disease. Leaves turning yellow and falling off and young shoots dying both denote root problems.

Poor soil structure is often a problem in new gardens, where heavy machinery has compacted the soil. Plant roots find it difficult to penetrate through compacted soil particles and water cannot drain away; plant growth is stunted or, in severe conditions, the plants will die. Another indicator of poor soil structure is the lack of worms in the soil, since they cannot survive anaerobic conditions. Cultivating the soil in wet conditions can also damage its structure, so be particularly careful when preparing areas to be seeded; newly seeded lawns can quickly become waterlogged in wet spells, poor growth and yellow or brown sod indicating that you have a problem. There is much that you can do to improve soil structure and suggestions are given in the chapter on Looking After The Garden, page 88.

Identifying the soil type and texture

The soil texture reflects the relative amounts of sand and clay particles in the soil. While not intended as a scientific analysis, the categories listed below indicate the range of soil types that may be found.

Clay soils Heavy soils are usually clay or clay loam. They will feel very smooth in texture and the fine particles are close grained; a handful of clay soil forms into a solid ball when molded in the hand. The advantages of clay soil are that it retains moisture and nutrients and can readily be improved by the addition of organic material and lime. When correctly cared for, clay soils are extremely fertile and make an excellent growing medium.

The amount of clay in the soil will determine its workability: the higher the proportion of clay, the more difficult the soil is to dig when very wet or very dry. When very wet it will stick to boots and tools and the structure is easily damaged. In prolonged dry spells the clay dries and shrinks, causing fissures in the ground. Damaged structure will mean poor drainage, less aeration and thus slower root penetration and decomposition of organic matter. But if the structure is retained, the soil will drain freely, encouraging root penetration and healthy plant growth. Being heavy and wet, clay soils take longer to warm up in the spring so root growth or the germination of seedlings may be slow.

Sandy soils These are composed of large particles that do not stick together; they feel coarse to the touch. The soil warms up quickly in spring and is easily worked but, being well drained, it dries out quickly after rain. The natural fertility of a sandy soil is low, as the nutrients tend to leach out readily, so it needs ample supplies of organic matter to keep it fertile and to help with moisture retention (see page 89). As the soil is well aerated, it stimulates vigorous root penetration and soil-organism activity, so any organic matter is rapidly decomposed. Plants self-seed readily in this soil. Many sandy soils are acid, due to the leaching of calcium, and therefore lend themselves to growing ericaceous plants; you should check the pH value first (see below).

Loam soils Loams comprise a mixture of clay and sandy soil particles. These soils are usually the most fertile and workable, open in texture and dark, sometimes almost black, in color. To the touch they are crumbly and feel slightly coarse. Loams usually have adequate drainage and good air penetration, encouraging vigorous rooting and plenty of soil-organism activity. Although loam is an excellent soil to work with, and you can grow a wide range of plants in it, its natural fertility will be enhanced by regular additions of organic matter in the form of manure or garden compost (see page 90).

Most established gardens will have a predominance of one soil type which may vary in different parts of the plot, according to previous management

The cream tulips, planted with golden feverfew and variegated periwinkle (Vinca major 'Variegata'), take advantage of the spring to flower before the full canopy of leaves appears on the cherry (Prunus species). Good soil preparation, involving shallow cultivation and the incorporation of organic matter, is vital to improve the soil's moisture retention in the shady area beneath a tree.

or because a developer has imported soil of a different type from the underlying soil. The type of soil will affect the range of plants which can be grown. Heavy, clay-based and low-lying soils which retain moisture throughout the year are suitable for damp loving subjects. True moisture lovers, such as astilbes, must be kept moist all the year round; if the clay has a tendency to dry out by the middle of summer they will become shriveled and brown. Heavy clay soil will be wet and lifeless in the winter and dry, hard-baked, cracked and totally unworkable in long, rainless summer spells. Soil improvement is the only solution (see page 88) to maximize the growing potential of a small garden.

Extremely sandy, alkaline or gravelly soil drains well and therefore tends to be dry. Plants that naturally enjoy dry conditions are the best choice here, as well as for hot, sunny aspects and raised beds which drain quickly. In a sunny, predominantly paved small garden, plants such as thyme and cotton lavender (*Santolina chamaecyparissus*) will thrive between paving slabs. Dry soil conditions are also found under trees or hedges where the foliage canopy prevents rain from reaching the soil and the tree or hedge roots consume vast quantities of moisture—a combination of factors which makes the soil below very dry and often starved of nutrients. Plants will need regular watering to help them to establish in these situations until they make enough root growth to become self-sufficient. Initial selection of the right plants for dry shade (see page 18) is essential for long-term success.

The condition of the soil

An overgrown, neglected small garden will undoubtedly be suffering from impoverished soil due to the few vigorous shrubs and trees that have taken over, extracting all the nutrients from the ground. Small gardens in new developments will often have very poor soil—indeed sometimes the builders just leave subsoil, the infertile layer found under the topsoil. It is virtually impossible to improve subsoil and my advice is to remove a layer of soil and relieve the compaction in the subsoil by forking it over to at least 12 in., before adding some well-rotted organic matter (see page 88) to improve the soil's fertility

and structure. Then import some good-quality top-soil to a minimum depth of 12 in. for planting and 6 in. for lawns.

Soil pollution is unusual and even new plots located on old industrial sites should have been cleaned of any chemical, oil or heavy-metal pollutants by the builder. All these products are toxic and will hinder or stop plant growth. Air pollution from exhaust fumes and industry can be a problem in many areas and will adversely affect plant growth. Some shrubs are more tolerant than others of polluted air and these include *Cotoneaster*, *Mahonia*, *Fatsia*, *Hedera*, *Pyracantha*, *Vinca*, *Euonymus*, *Forsythia*, *Pernettya* and *Sorbus*.

The degree of acidity or alkalinity of the soil must be considered before plant selection is made. This is measured on a scale known as pH: to test the pH of your soil, obtain a soil testing kit from a garden center, then take random samples from different parts of the garden. A neutral soil, represented by pH 7, is suitable for growing a wide range of plants. Soils with a reading above pH 7 are alkaline; lumps of chalk in the ground will indicate a very alkaline soil. Plants such as *Jasminum nudiflorum*, *Daphne odora*, *Garrya elliptica*, *Osmanthus* × *burkwoodii*, *Choisya ternata* and *Juniperus*, *Ceanothus*, *Lavandula* and *Spiraea* will all grow well in alkaline soils. An acid soil, often associated with peaty soil and some sandy soils, has a pH below 7 and will host a very different range of plants: acid-loving shrubs such as rhododendrons, azaleas and heathers all flourish in these conditions. Other acid-loving evergreens suitable for a small garden include *Camellia*, *Skimmia* and *Gaultheria mucronata* cultivars, along with the deciduous hydrangeas, including *Hydrangea macrophylla* cultivars and *H*. 'Preziosa.'

For a small garden I recommend working with the soil you have, using plants that will thrive on your particular soil and so be naturally healthy and therefore less prone to disease and cultivation problems. But if you are determined to grow plants which will not thrive in your soil, include a raised bed in your garden design (see page 59) and fill this with imported topsoil of the correct pH. Another alternative is to plant such species in containers filled with an appropriate compost.

The microclimate

General weather patterns vary widely on a global scale, according to the part of the world you live in and thus your proximity to the equator. More specifically, your location within a country will impose typical weather patterns, influenced by factors such as altitude, proximity to the coast and prevailing winds. But the effects of the weather are further influenced by even more localized effects, known as microclimates. However small the garden, you will find that it breaks down into several different climatic zones, comprising effects from wind, sun, shade, rain and frost.

A thorough understanding of your garden's microclimate will enable you to select suitable plants for different positions, and ensure that they grow healthily. However appropriate the size, shape or color of the plant you like, there is no point in including it in the design if the growing conditions are wrong. A south-facing wall is always warmer than a north-facing fence for example, and this is where sun-loving climbers should be grown. In an exposed garden, if you walk around on a windy day you will discover which areas feel most sheltered from the prevailing wind. These are the spots for more tender plants as well as for seating areas.

Sun and shade

Throughout the year, the height of the sun in the sky alters significantly, being lowest in winter, and the length of the day can vary by up to eight hours, being longest at midsummer. This means the points at which the sun strikes early in the morning and late in the afternoon will change from season to season, as well as the proportion of the garden the sun encompasses. While a compass reading will indicate the aspect of a garden, it does not record changing shade patterns so you should watch how your garden is affected by the movement of the sun throughout the seasons and note down the results.

A shady spot in early spring can be in more or less full sun by the summer. These summertime hot spots can then spend several winter months without any warmth at all, when the sun does not climb high enough in the sky or is obstructed by tall buildings.

In my small garden, which has many different climatic environments, even some sun-loving plants on the south border find it a struggle to survive through the winter, mainly because the sun never dries out the soil or the plant foliage, and both remain damp and cold. Careful selection of plants is vital. The best plants for this situation need to enjoy hot, dry sites (do not be tempted to use damp-loving species); to help overcome winter wetness, the soil should be made as light and well drained as possible by the addition of organic matter and some sand or grit (see page 88).

By contrast, a north-facing border or indeed a whole garden surrounded by buildings, high walls or tall evergreens can be in full or part shade for the entire year, calling for a completely different range of plants. Trees can also cast permanent shade and the best choice of plants for both situations is undoubtedly shade-lovers. The band of shade cast by a tree will vary according to the season. Plants on the south side and those further away from the tree will get a little more light than those directly underneath and species suitable for semi-shade can then be introduced. Deciduous trees which lose their leaves in the winter allow sunlight to filter through the branches and warm the soil below the tree, making this an ideal site for small winter bulbs. Few plants thrive in conditions of deep shade.

Wind

Strong winds have a damaging effect on plants, often a very localized one. Some shelter or form of protection will be required to prevent damage; if the prevailing wind is westerly, for example, some protection will be required on the west boundary to create sheltered spaces for plants. Gardens in cities generally seem more protected but wind tunnels created by tall buildings can be harmful. When the wind is funneled between walls or buildings, these confined spaces increase its velocity, often resulting in physical damage to plants, such as browning or wind scorch; young evergreen leaves in winter are particularly vulnerable. Planting hardy trees and shrubs as barriers will slow the wind's passage and provide a degree of localized protection. For example, if you plant a tall, hardy shrub such as

PLANTS FOR
DRY SHADE
Alchemilla mollis
Aucuba japonica
  'Variegata'
Bamboos
Bergenia
Hedera helix helix
  (green-leaved species
  and cultivars)
Ilex
Iris foetidissima
Prunus laurocerasus
Vinca minor
  'Bowles' Variety'

PLANTS FOR
MOIST SHADE
Ajuga reptans
Ferns
Helleborus
Hosta
Osmanthus decorus
Viburnum davidii

Forsythia suspensa to receive the brunt of the wind, and a medium-sized shrub such as *Prunus laurocerasus* 'Zabelliana' in its lee, then a smaller, tender plant such as *Convolvulus cneorum* can be tucked in their shelter. Each plant affords the other some protection, even within a very small group.

Securely erected trellis panels positioned to break the strength of the wind give some protection without presenting a solid barrier (see page 53). Solid walls block the wind but create turbulence and the wind can then be very damaging some distance away, on what seems to be the sheltered side. A more open, planted barrier, by contrast, filters the wind: a line of shrubs allows the wind to dissipate its speed gradually, creating less turbulence; the reduced wind speed is felt over a distance of up to ten times the height of the barrier.

The altitude of a garden will also affect the microclimate—the higher a site, the colder it usually is and the more prone to damaging winds. Roof and balcony gardens are often very exposed and a pergola or other structure using overhead beams will provide shelter and shade. A permeable screen such as trellis provides an ideal windbreak on a roof since its open nature reduces the force of the wind, while allowing some through. Planting on the trellis will further filter the wind. Ensure that any trellis is firmly fixed so that it will not blow down in strong gusts. An alternative is to fix clear glass screens on the windward side, to give the plants protection and make it more pleasant to sit out. In high-level gardens without shade, the combination of wind and relentless hot summer sun has a desiccating effect on plant foliage, and a range of plants able to withstand the contrast of hot sun in summer and cold, damaging winds in winter must grown (see the list on page 54).

Coastal gardens not only have wind to contend with but also the effect of salt carried on the wind. A grouping of plants for shelter will be needed to break the effect of the wind and create protected corners. For gardens on the coast, select salt- and wind-tolerant plants, for example, ash *(Fraxinus excelsior)* and species of *Griselinia* and *Escallonia*. Due to the conditions in a coastal garden, plant growth tends to be stunted and even the ash will probably grow to only 12–20 ft., making it suitable for a small plot. If you have only a tiny paved space, the best solution is to furnish it with tolerant plants, such as *Viola tricolor*, *Silene maritima*, osteospermums and mesembryanthemums, in pots during the summer months, when conditions are more favorable.

Frost

Frost pockets, or areas where particularly cold air gathers and cannot escape, may be evident in the confined space of a small garden. Avoid planting fruit here as late frosts will damage the blossom and reduce the fruit crop. Do not plant early-flowering shrubs such as magnolias and camellias in these areas as they will suffer from frost-burnt flowers; the early morning sun would melt any frost covering the plants too quickly. If you have an east-facing border, protect more tender plants during winter and early spring to avoid the early morning sun. As frost disperses, the cold air tends to move downhill and drain away, but in an enclosed garden at the bottom of a hill, frost will be prevented from escaping; this problem can sometimes be overcome by creating a gap in the boundary hedge or fence. If this cannot be done, then particularly hardy plants must be selected. The overhanging branches of a large tree will reduce heat loss from the soil and thus reduce the incidence of frost in that area, and overhead structures such as pergolas and arbors will also afford some localized protection.

Rain

All plants need water and if there is plenty of rain you may be lulled into a false sense of security. But in a small space surrounded by walls or fences and protected by other buildings or a large tree, the full benefit of rain is never received. On the sheltered side of a wall, the soil tends to be dry, whereas the soil on the windward side receives more rain. Well-drained soils, perhaps overlying gravel, tend to be dry in every season, although the addition of organic matter will improve their moisture retention (see page 88). Even small areas of more moisture-retentive soil can be permanently shielded from rain if they are under overhanging eaves or projecting windows. Drought-tolerant plants such as rosemary, *Acanthus*, *Ceanothus* and *Lavatera* will survive in sun-baked, dry soil.

*A silver birch (*Betula pendula*), Miscanthus sinensis and the leyland cypress (*×Cupressocyparis leylandii*) create a foliage screen which affords this roof garden a degree of shelter. A wisteria clambers up overhead beams, giving dappled shade to the seating area. Regular watering will be essential to counteract moisture loss through the leaves in this exposed, sunny site.*

Drawing a site plan

Drawing a plan of your existing garden will enable you to put on to paper the information collected through the seasons, along with the measurements of your site. Triangulation (see right) is a reliable method of measuring your garden and positioning the existing features in it. To convert the actual dimensions into a smaller unit, work on a piece of graph paper or use a scale ruler. A scale of 1:20 or 1:50—that is, one yard on the paper representing 20 yards or 50 yards on the ground—gives a good size plan that you can draw up on a 16 × 23 in. sheet of paper. The squares on graph paper can be used instead of a scale ruler: each inch square could represent 1 yard on the ground.

Include on your plan the position of the ground-floor doors and windows (denoting the way they open), inspection covers, drains, known services and garden structures. It is essential to position all features correctly on the plan to make sure of your viewpoints and to make the right estimations for materials. Seeing the shape of the garden on paper will give you a more accurate picture of the plot. Some planting or design in the garden may have already deceived the eye and made it appear longer or wider than you thought. Even if only part of the garden is to be reorganized it is still important to

draw it out on paper and to include any other areas which are affected, whether visually or physically. The part you are altering may be in view from a window, for example, so the position of the house needs to be clearly indicated in relation to this.

Plot the spread of an existing tree's canopy and the diameter of the trunk on the plan and note shadows cast at different times of the day. Using a compass, mark the north point to remind you of the sun's position through the seasons, so that you site borders and features in the right places, to give your plants sun or shade, depending on their requirements. Denote views, both pleasant and unsightly, to ensure that the design takes account of these; look outside your boundaries as well, noting factors that affect your garden, such as the overhanging canopy of a neighbor's tree or the height of an adjacent wall, which will block out the sun at certain times of day.

Before embarking on a new layout, look at the garden from the house, from both upstairs and downstairs rooms. Ask yourself which view is the most important and how can focal points be linked with the views? Also assess views from the garden back toward the house—perhaps an attractive door or window needs framing by climbing plants. The perspective will be very different from up- and

Measuring levels using pegs

Place a short peg at the highest point, then drive longer pegs into the ground wherever there is a distinct change of level, or at fixed points across the plot (spaced no more than 10 ft. apart), until all the pegs appear level. . Lay a scaffold board across the tops of the pegs, place a spirit level on it and adjust the height of the pegs either side until the bubble is in the center. When every peg is level, measure the distance from the top of each peg to ground level. The difference indicates the change of level from one point to the next.

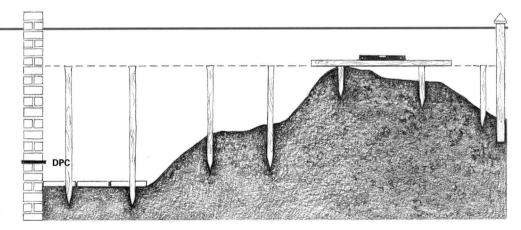

While the peg at the highest point is level with the ground, the peg on the patio is 2 ft. long. The highest point in this garden

is therefore 2 ft. above the level of the patio—that is 1½ ft. above the damp-proof course (DPC).

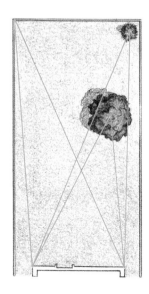

A small change of level in this plot has been used to create three separate spaces within the garden. A pair of clipped boxes (Buxus sempervirens) in terra-cotta pots emphasize the first division and frame the entrance to the middle, grassed "room," while the marble statue peeping out of the greenery at the far end provides a focal point in the third, paved space.

TRIANGULATION
Select and measure one of the house walls to use as your baseline. Take a tape and measure the distance from either end of this straight line to each component of the garden, forming a triangle; note the dimensions on a piece of paper. Measure all existing structures, features, plants and borders. To position them on your scale plan, you will need to convert the measurements to the scale you are using, and set a pair of compasses to the radius of one, then the other measurement; make an arc from each known point, such as either end of the house wall, and where they intersect marks the accurate position of the feature.

downstairs—place a statue or birdbath in the garden and look at the effect from both viewpoints. A sloping garden running away from view will, when seen from a downstairs room, appear to be diminishing in size, whereas a terraced garden sloping uphill will appear as a series of walls on top of one another. Any terraces must therefore not be too high and dominant—softening with plants will help. If you look along your paper plan, holding the edge near eye level, it will help to give an idea of the effects your design is creating and the way shapes change when seen from different angles.

Measuring a change of level

In a garden that is more or less flat, it is not essential to measure the levels; when laying paving, simply check that the fall is away from the building by using a spirit level. But for a garden with a definite slope you will need accurate measurements of the changes of level to determine, for example, the height and number of steps needed, or the height of a possible retaining wall or raised bed. It is important to measure any change of level against a fixed point

which cannot be altered, and record all levels relative to this. The damp-proof course in the house walls is a very suitable point since any surface adjacent to the house wall must always be two brick courses below the damp-proof course. Other levels which will remain constant may include boundary fences, shed bases and trees and shrubs which you wish to retain. It is important to avoid raising ground levels above the top of the fence gravel boards since this will considerably reduce the life of the timber, and soil levels must not be raised around a tree trunk or shrub since this may kill the plant.

The simplest way to assess the levels within a small garden is to knock in pegs, using lengths of wood from a lumber merchant, as illustrated below left; use a scaffold board, or similar thick board that does not warp, to lay across them. Another method is to extend a hose down from a fixed high point and run water into it; raise the lower end of the hose until no water flows out and yet the hose is full of water to the very end. The height of this above the low point you are measuring indicates the difference in the level from the fixed high point.

Using the garden

The working area and shed are cleverly tucked away behind a panel of purpose-designed trellis, disguised all year round with Hedera algeriensis *'Gloire de Marengo,' behind which is* Weigela florida *'Albovariegata.'* Campanula portenschlagiana *tumbles attractively over the path. Even the washing-line post blends unobtrusively into the scene.*

Having drawn a plan of the existing garden, consider carefully your practical requirements before making any final decisions about a new or modified layout. Make a checklist of all your needs—for example a sitting area, a storage area and any working areas, such as a compost heap—that accurately reflects the role the garden will play in your everyday life. These areas will need to be allocated a realistic amount of space on the final plan (see page 29).

A table and four chairs will fit comfortably on a patio of 27 to 34 sq. ft. and allow space for a large container or group of smaller pots. But it may be more appropriate to create more than one paved space. Always consider the position of a patio in relation to the garden's aspect. Sun lovers will want the main seating area to be in full sun, whether this is adjacent to the house or at the far end of the garden. Those who prefer to be in shade may site a patio under a tree or in a northerly corner, or build an overhead canopy for dappled shade.

Paths will be essential to any design, whether they take the form of stepping stones across a lawn or border, are partly integrated with a terrace, or connect different areas of the garden. A minimum comfortable width for a path is 2 ft.

A shed may be needed for storing garden tools and equipment if there is not a garage; do allow sufficient space for access with lawn mower, bicycles or garden furniture. There are two types of building available, one with an apex roof which has two pitches and the other with a one-pitch sloping roof. A single-pitch roof reduces the overall height and it can be more easily disguised with trellis or planting. Position the shed in a part of the garden out of view from the main living space, if possible, or in an area where plants do not grow easily, for example in dry shade. Plants climbing up a trellis, a fast-growing shrub or espalier fruit trees will all help to screen the structure from view. Evergreen foliage gives a more solid barrier. Screening will inevitably be required for trash cans too. Storage space for these must be accessible from the house and wheeled cans are best located near to the collection point.

Providing a greenhouse with ample sunlight will be difficult in many small gardens but this may be a priority for the keen gardener; it could be of a decorative construction if it cannot be hidden away. A small cold frame is less obtrusive and more easily sited and will enable the enthusiast to grow small annuals from seed. Tender plants may also be given some winter protection here.

A paved storage or work area is always useful, space permitting. A compost bin will help with limited recycling of garden and kitchen waste, providing some organic matter for soil improvement (see page 88). A shredder reduces the volume of bulky garden waste before composting and is a worthwhile investment for environment-conscious gardeners. It is often impossible to conceal a washing line or rotary clothes drier in a small space but a retractable line can be wound up again after use and a rotary drier put away. Locate them where the washing will not blow against too much planting.

This small brick-paved garden accommodates the needs of small children without losing any of its beauty. A cover should be placed on the sand pit when not in use.

ESSENTIAL TOOLS

A first-time gardener must decide which tools are truly indispensable. Always buy the best quality you can afford.

● **Spade** For digging, cultivation and planting.

● **Fork** For ground preparation and aerating the soil.

● **Hoe** For weeding around plants and incorporating fertilizer; choose the flat-bladed Dutch hoe.

● **Hand trowel** For planting bedding, small plants and bulbs.

● **Border fork** For hand weeding in confined areas, raised beds and planted containers.

● **Pruning shears** For dead-heading, pruning and clipping/shaping.

● **Rake** For creating a tillage, scarifying lawns and collecting fallen leaves.

● **Hand shears** For cutting a small hedge, edging a lawn and trimming some shrubs.

● **Hose and watering can** For all watering, including pots.

A lawn will be high on the list of priorities for some, either as an open play space or for aesthetic effect. Evaluate the growing conditions and be realistic about its potential success before making a final decision. A lawn that does not grow well will be anathema to a gardener who envisaged a bowling-green finish. Guidance is given in the next chapter (see page 47) on the best type of lawn for different uses and different growing conditions. It is good design practice to lay lawns or grass paths in multiples of your mower width.

If the front garden needs to incorporate a car parking space, minimize its impact by designing an imaginatively shaped paved surface, not just a car-shaped rectangle. Allow room for opening car doors on at least one side and avoid building low walls which may catch an opening door. Planting will soften the overall picture and provide limited screening. Placing a focal point away from the parked car will direct the eye elsewhere. An attractive front door and porch with a matching pair of well-planted containers will also successfully detract attention

from the car. Above all, front gardens must be welcoming, and not just a parking space.

Add any more personal requirements to your list and ensure that it is complete so the final design is not spoiled by the addition of afterthoughts. Consider the maintenance of the garden at this stage, before getting carried away with a labor-intensive list. Rock gardens and ponds containing fish and plants require regular attention by someone knowledgeable. The type of plants selected will significantly affect the level of maintenance required: a garden with predominantly slow-growing shrubs, for example *Choisya ternata* 'Sundance,' *Hebe albicans* 'Red Edge' and *Skimmia japonica*, will require the least maintenance, those planted with annuals the most. From experience and by studying books, compile your own individual plant care notes to get an idea of the after-care required (see page 94).

Making a wish list

It is a good idea to supplement your list of practical requirements with a list of features and effects you would like to have in your garden, including ideas gleaned while visiting or reading about other gardens. Take time to mull over your aspirations, before finally reaching a shorter list of desired features. This wish list may include a water feature in some form, a pergola, arbor, statue, containers, seat, or a wildlife corner, as well as specific plants or plant groups. Try to rationalize your ideas before you start drawing the sketch plan, so that the garden does not become a confused mass. It is important to have a perception of the style, size and shape of each feature or focal point to be included. You may already have the seat or statue and therefore know its dimensions; indeed, I often specify "statue" on a garden design and know that it must be of fairly specific dimensions and of a certain material to create the right feel. Then comes the fun of going around garden centers and shows or browsing through catalogs looking for the right piece. Beware of buying from pictures without further research, as this can be misleading.

Considering a budget

***Philadelphus coronarius*
'Aureus'**
*The mock orange was named
by the Greeks after Ptolomy
Philadelphus, King of
Egypt. Linnaeus records
Philadelphus coronarius as
a native of Verona, Italy,
though a more likely habitat
is the Near East, where its
pliable branches, covered in
citrus-scented blossom, were
used to make coronets.*

Before getting carried away with a design, look at the costs of the various elements in it. Visit garden centers and hardware stores to assess the relative price of different materials. As a rule of thumb, hard landscaping, which includes all paths, walls and paved areas, is the most costly item within the garden and soft landscaping (the plants and possibly a lawn) a much smaller proportion: allow roughly 75 percent of the total cost for hard landscaping and 25 percent for the soft landscaping. It is almost impossible to give figures for the average overall cost of a new garden because every situation is so different, but as a starting point think of the cost of a new family car or a new kitchen and compare that to the cost of a small garden. It is always possible to phase the work so that an increased budget can be stretched over a longer period of time.

Certain tasks are more economically carried out together, utilizing the equipment while it is on site. The hard landscape elements, such as the patio, walls and shed base will all require footings to provide solid, firm foundations without which walls will move and paving will crack or subside. This process entails digging out the soil to a suitable depth and then backfilling with a hardcore or cement sub-base, before laying bricks or paving slabs. Once the sub-base is laid, it forms a dry, level surface and if funds are limited it will suffice until you can afford the paving. In my garden, for example, the most essential stage was to redesign and pave the patio because it was in daily use. This work, together with a flight of steps leading to the door and an integral small raised bed adjacent to the garage wall, logically constituted the first phase, while paving elsewhere in the garden was left for a later date.

Keeping the costs down

Savings on labor costs will be made by designing the dimensions of your patio and paths in units of the selected paving, thereby avoiding costly cuts and joints. Do not, however, lose the flow and overall concept of the design by compromising on cost-saving cuts. The cost of surfacing varies from the lowest, grass and planting, to that of bark and gravel and then paving. This ranges in price, with natural stone, clay bricks and pavers at the top end.

Changes of level can be costly, since retaining walls use a lot of material both above and below ground. The higher the wall, the wider the construction needs to be, particularly of the footings, for stability and therefore the more expensive it becomes. Timber retaining walls are generally marginally cheaper than brick, provided they blend with the overall design, and a grass or planted bank, space permitting, is the least expensive way of changing level. And if it is necessary to increase soil levels above the base of a wooden fence, concrete gravel boards can be used to do the retaining and are less expensive than brick. The soil will cover them.

Alongside the price considerations for surfaces, you need to think carefully about the practical use of the space. If the garden is to be used for a lot of outdoor entertaining, a solid surface is the best option. Where there are small children in the family, then an area of lawn for play may be required, as well as a paved patio area. To maximize growing space, a graveled area will combine hard surfacing with an excellent medium for integrating planting.

Thorough preparation of the ground is a major task that has to be undertaken before planting. If time is limited, this could be carried out by a contractor, but if funds are the restricting factor, you can save money by doing this yourself. Soil preparation is extremely important and must not be skimped (see page 88). Phasing the planting will also spread costs—even in a small garden the cost of plants can equate to that of a new wool carpet for a large room. Instant gardens are very appealing and planting mature trees and shrubs certainly helps to achieve this, but large plants which have taken a long time to grow in someone else's garden or nursery are much more expensive. Incorporating one or two mature specimens may be sufficient to give some immediate structure to the garden. Using ready-grown clipped or topiary specimens as focal points, even in pots, are excellent for this purpose.

**BRIEFING A
PROFESSIONAL
DESIGNER OR
CONTRACTOR**

- Always be specific
about your requirements
- Ensure that everything
is put in writing
- Agree on start and
completion dates
- Make sure the contract
includes a clause stating
that the site will be
cleared and left clean and
tidy at the end of the job
- Make the main
contractor responsible for
any sub-contracted labor
and their standard of work
- Check that the
contractor has adequate
insurance coverage.

Professional help

If you feel that the design or redesign of the garden is beyond your capabilities then you might consider employing a professional. One discussion with an experienced garden designer may be all you need to progress alone. Otherwise the designer will proceed to survey the garden and produce an accurate scale plan of the existing site, noting all the relevant existing features and factors such as soil type and aspect. This information will be used to prepare a draft design plan which has the proposed new layout for your garden, showing the position of patio, paths, lawn, flower beds, trees and other structural features. Modifications can be discussed at this stage.

Preparation of detailed planting plans, construction detail drawings and monitoring the contractors on site are all optional extras. With your newly drawn plans, you may wish to build the garden yourself or employ a skilled landscape contractor directly. Alternatively, most professional garden designers will recommend contractors and monitor the garden construction, including the planting. Another approach is to draw up your own design for the garden's layout and planting, and employ a landscape contractor to build it for you. This contractor will usually be willing to work on an option basis, if you just need help with the hard landscaping, the soil preparation or the planting, which may involve moving your existing stock around. Those preparing their own designs may still approach a garden designer to draw up a planting plan.

Selecting a designer is an exacting task. How can you be sure of finding the right person, whose knowledge and capabilities are up to your project? My advice is to choose a designer with good training and some previous experience, so make sure yours is not the first garden to be built. It is just as important to select a designer with creative flair and the ability to interpret your wishes, and to end up with a feasible design. Garden improvements can be equated with major house renovation in both time scale and cost and it is important to feel confident that they are being competently carried out, with contractors who respect the invasion of your privacy.

Unless you are following a personal recommendation, the initial selection of a garden designer or contractor might be through a professional body, which requires high standards and carries out work inspection before members can join. Or you could contact someone recommended through a reputable local garden center. Arrange to meet the designer or contractor before going any further: it is vital to feel comfortable with the person you will be working with, so that your ideas or design are interpreted sympathetically. Then take up references and follow these through by looking at some completed projects. Make sure at least one of them is a few years old so that you can assess the longevity of the standard of workmanship and the quality of materials. Are the joints in the brickwork and the paving regular, is the brick clean or has it been carelessly smeared with mortar? Are the paved areas level, with no uneven surfaces, and laid so that puddles of rainwater do not collect? Does the pond leak?

The quality of plants is a little more difficult to assess unless you look at newly planted stock, because over a season they will grow and change and the health and shape of the plant will reflect the level of after-care. Unhealthy, poor-looking plants may have or have had pests and diseases. Visit the nursery from which the designer or contractor is buying the plants: buying from a reputable nursery or garden center helps to ensure good-quality specimens.

Charges for professional designers generally reflect their experience and knowledge; you should bear in mind that a less experienced designer may lack expertise when dealing with problem areas or with contractors. Similarly, when assessing the contractor's quotations, do not necessarily opt for the cheapest. The quality of workmanship is always related to price and the end result will to a large extent reflect what you pay. So, aim to strike at a level of competence and quality that fulfils your needs and is within your budget; otherwise phase the work to enable you to select a top-quality company.

Understanding design principles

To make the most of a small garden it helps to understand a few basic design rules. This will ensure that even the smallest alteration to a garden's layout, for example changing the shape of a border or adding a statue, will enhance the overall design. The aim of good design is to please the senses and the simplicity of a coherent, uncluttered garden plan will provide a relaxing atmosphere, whereas a jumble of contradictory lines and patterns, furnished with many different features, will look piecemeal and lose the flow. Recognizing these few basic principles is the key to developing your own small garden into a pleasing, balanced space in proportion with its surroundings.

Natural materials for surfaces and features combine sympathetically to create a formal, uncluttered design. A balance is achieved between the open spaces (or voids) of lawn and water and the structural elements created by foliage-clad arches and pillars, trees and wall shrubs (the mass).

Harmony

In the style you develop for your garden, you should aim to create continuity with both the surroundings and the house. Plants and materials should match or blend so that the whole is in harmony. For example,

a design with a strong Mediterranean feel, using plants such as *Phormium* and *Yucca* and colored mosaic floor tiles, would look quite out of keeping adjacent to a black-and-white cottage. But selecting a material found in the house construction to use in the garden would give continuity and a small black-and-white summerhouse, or white-painted trellis supporting old-fashioned roses, would be far more appropriate here than a Mediterranean-style garden. Brick and stone both make ideal materials for harmonizing the house and the garden. Do not be put off by a builder telling you there are no suitable products available: a determined search at local quarries, stone specialists and brick "libraries" will invariably produce results. Unity of design will generally be maintained by keeping things simple and not over-designing the space by introducing too many focal points or features whose combined effect will only cause confusion.

To achieve harmony in a small space, choose two or at the most three materials for surfacing and structures such as boundaries, so that the effect is not cluttered; too many different materials will be visually confusing and will dilute the overall theme. If you have brick walls, for example, you might choose natural stone paving with brick detailing incorporated in it. The type of surface chosen will affect the garden's overall style. Smooth, precise lines, as found in stone or concrete slabs, will indicate formality, whereas rough surfaces such as gravel or bark can be more informal and flowing.

Patterns created by the line and arrangement of paving units can further enhance the atmosphere of the garden. For example, a small, enclosed sunny courtyard with whitewashed walls would have a sophisticated feel when paved with polished or smooth-finished paving laid in regular lines. Brick walls and a graveled surface, broken up by stepping stones, would feel more informal. A Japanese-style garden works well in a small space, its inherent harmony creating an attractive picture (see page 39). The simple composition of evergreen plants with bricks, gravel and possibly water is very restful.

Scale and proportion

The garden design must be in scale with the surroundings and the proportions considered in every plane to ensure that the plants and features selected are appropriate for the space. Your two-dimensional plan must be envisaged in three dimensions either in your mind, or by drawing your design over a photograph of an existing view. Perspective can be used to create different design effects and if you play around with different possibilities for placing features and focal points, you will usually know instinctively which arrangement achieves the best balance and proportion. For instance, a substantial pot placed immediately outside the patio doors will look very large in a small garden when seen from the house; however, when moved halfway down the garden to a lower-level paved area it will appear much smaller. A pergola always looks better if the height and width are more or less equal.

Ultimate plant sizes must also be in proportion to the garden. A large sculptural plant can be stunning in its own right but becomes absurd if it is out of balance with the rest of the design. When selecting plants, note their size in five, ten and twenty years to assess their suitability. The overhead mass of a very tall tree can be out of proportion in a small garden, completely dwarfing and shrouding everything else. There are no hard and fast rules about scale and proportion and every situation will need to be addressed individually. I find one of the most effective ways to clarify the picture is to create a vertical element by holding up a cane or surveying pole in the selected parts of the garden. Imagine this as the tree or feature you are considering, and observe the different effects from pertinent viewpoints.

The width of the border, paths and steps should be as broad as possible and yet in balance with the house. If levels permit, give step treads generous dimensions, never less than 18 in., and make the risers low, preferably between 4½–6 in., to give the feel of a leisurely pace. Very shallow steps can be dangerous, however, especially to the poor-sighted,

and on a shallow slope, a better solution would be to make the garden into a series of generous terraces on different levels, each with its own character (see the picture on page 21).

The size of paving units will affect the overall scale. Very small units can look fussy whereas extremely large slabs can be overpowering in an intimate space, making it appear smaller. A drive paved in clay or concrete pavers in front of a brick house can look overdone and busy, with a myriad small units. By using some larger-unit paving, and integrating it with brick to match the house, the whole composition will become more sympathetic.

The whitewashed walls and strong pattern of the paving give this garden a contemporary feel. Granite cobblestones lend themselves to a circular design, while the textured pavers create a strong grid pattern. The bold foliage of Gunnera manicata, *with box and bamboo, reinforces the contemporary style.*

Shapes and balance

Different shapes create a sense of either movement or repose. Circles, hexagons and shapes with equal proportions are restful on the eye, causing one to pause and relax. Long, slim shapes, as in a narrow path, have a strong sense of movement. In between there are oval and rectangular shapes which have a more neutral quality and therefore create less strong effects. Use the elements of your garden design—including the borders, trees and shrubs as well as the seats and pots—to create well-proportioned shapes that are in balance with one another and which counterbalance the voids; these are the essential static spaces created by lawn, open water and paved or flat surfaces. If you wish to bring a sense of movement to the design, create a series of focal points linked by paths and open spaces. This sounds very grand but even in a small plot the composition will have open spaces that can be separated from each other by tall plants, arches or trellis. For example, from the patio adjacent to the house the eye can be led through an arch to an open space containing a focal point, from where a hint of another "room" may be visible, tempting you to investigate.

The vertical elements of the garden will also help to create its overall shape and balance. Plants may be too small to fulfill their role at first but given time and growth the balance will establish itself. Planting above eye level becomes a dramatic feature which attracts attention. For example, a dark columnar evergreen or a well-clipped formal hedge create strong horizontal and vertical lines and the shadows cast add to the drama. Strong shapes like these can be used sculpturally; their design might reflect that of the piers supporting the porch or a balustrade outside a balcony window. Tall planting adjacent to a path will make it appear narrower, whereas a strip of grass beside it will make the path seem wider. Using plant shapes and color in repeat groupings will add balance to the design. Try to balance the opposite boundaries: a solid wall on one side with an open boundary on the other will look awkward. Use a softer boundary material such as a fence (see page 51) if you wish to retain openness, or use two walls or solid fences to create a sense of enclosure.

This historic outbuilding is successfully incorporated into the author's design for this garden. A water rill links the main garden to the small courtyard and the house beyond the outbuilding, while the circular water features create a balance between the two spaces. Honeysuckle (Lonicera japonica) and Wisteria floribunda 'Macrobotrys,' planted in the ground and trained up against the walls of the outbuilding, soften the structure. Hosta 'Thomas Hogg' provides attractively variegated foliage.

The components of the garden can be used to manipulate views beyond the boundary—strong elements such as an imposing statue tend to stop the eye, whereas softer elements, for example an informal pool, and softer colors like blue will lead the eye further down the garden. Wide-open views have less impact than those to which the eye is subtly directed, for example, through an arch or along a path leading to a gate. If the view is unattractive or bleak or there is no view at all, you will want the whole garden to focus inward. Create a solid boundary and use well-placed shapes and focal points to draw the eye inward.

Shaping your plot

No two small gardens are alike, but many of us have to deal with conventionally shaped plots, perhaps long and narrow, rectangular or square. Some garden plots will be flat, others on a slope or cut into a hillside. The boundaries themselves influence our perception of the garden's shape but skillful design and softening the boundary fences with planting can do much to deceive the eye. There are no specific design rules relating to garden shape but certain treatments work better than others for a particular outline (see the plans on pages 30–5).

Arranging the garden

When you have gathered all the information about the existing plot and put it onto a site plan (see page 20), you will be thinking about how you wish to use the garden. Once you feel ready, you can start putting pen to paper to bring the practical and aspirational elements together to create the new garden on the bones of the existing one. If you plan to extend the house or add a conservatory at a future date, I recommend that you add this to your plan before arranging the garden since a new conservatory in a small space can upset the balance of a design. Even if it is several years before the alterations take place, at least the end result will be well designed and not a compromise.

When you have indicated different areas of the garden and their practical use (see below), start to draw shapes and create patterns which link them together. The most important aim is to maximize your garden's potential and simplicity of design will invariably produce the most harmonious result. Using interlocking shapes will give the design cohesion while linking the different elements. Patterns with flowing curves and long, narrow, straight-edged shapes will introduce movement. However, do not use expansive serpentine curves in a small space, as they will be totally out of scale. You should also avoid patterns which create awkward, impracti-cal corners. Try to incorporate all the existing features of the garden in such a way that they become an integral part of the new design.

As soon as all the shapes are connected and you are satisfied with the style that has started to develop, the content can become more specific and detail may be added. You can now select paving materials to fit in with your design, measuring and adjusting the layout to ensure that it can be laid in multiple units. Fences, steps, structural planting and other features can be added to the plan, which at this stage will become an accurate working drawing.

Trying out the design

Once the design is complete, it is a good idea to peg it out on the ground to make certain that it works in reality and to help you visualize the end result. A hosepipe or piece of colored string can be laid to designate curved paths or lawn edges, a tall cane stuck in the ground to represent a tree and an existing pot or statue placed in its proposed new home, to start to paint the picture. A few old bricks laid down temporarily to represent the path will give you some idea of how it will look when finally constructed. Live with the shapes for a while, and alter any areas that look uncomfortable. Whether you construct the garden all in one go or spend several years achieving your objective, you now have a coherent design toward which to work.

Formulating the design

The simplest way of drawing the design is to lay a piece of heavy-grade tracing paper over your original site plan and, in pencil, allocate suitable areas, writing in patio, shed, lawn and so on where you feel they will be most appropriate and effective. Most features and other components will have a logical place within the garden, but if you are in any doubt, leave them aside until the picture becomes clearer. At this early stage the aim is to create a visually satisfying pattern which works well in your small space.

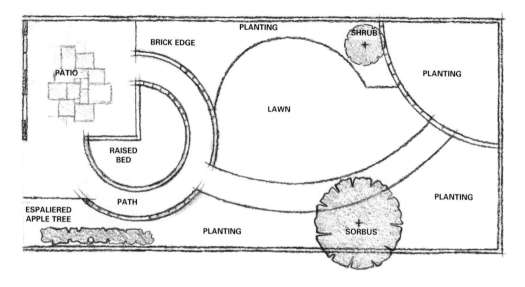

The long, narrow garden

How you deal with a long, narrow plot depends on whether you wish to camouflage the shape or accentuate it. It is easy to create movement within this shape since it inherently leads the eye on. The design can accentuate this by creating a series of "rooms" linked by well-placed focal points to draw you from one space to the next. At no time must focal points vie for attention or the design will become too busy and confuse the eye. By placing the room "entrances" off-center, the design optically lengthens the view by creating spaces of varying width and increasing the apparent length of the garden. Varying the width of paved and planted areas also alters the perception of the garden's overall width.

The plan shown below is for a garden measuring 51 ft. long by 15 ft. wide. Planting schemes for the areas marked A and B are illustrated opposite, as they appear in midsummer.

Year-round shrub planting will provide permanent structure between rooms; for example, dome-shaped evergreens create a division without being too high.

It may be preferable to emphasize the linear shape. The traditional path down the center, with lawn and borders on each side, is not a very imaginative way of dealing with the garden. An off-center path will still accentuate the length; wider stopping spaces for a seat or other feature will add interest en route and informal planting will soften the edges of the paved surface. The length can be accentuated further by laying brick paving in a running bond down the garden, the pace reduced by incorporating cross-bonding or a change of surface.

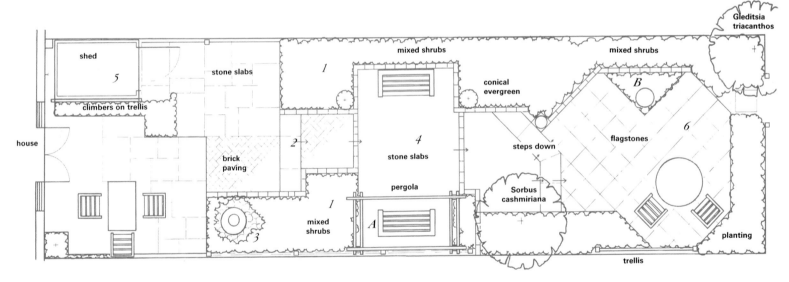

1 Trellis, walls, hedges or just tall plants can divide the plot into areas or "rooms," each with its own character—but you should avoid creating very small, cramped spaces out of proportion with the rest of the house and garden.
2 Some low-level planting across the width of the garden, or a step or two down into a sunken space, will have the effect of breaking the view and creating an intimate space.
3 Placing a water feature such as a Minoan urn as a focal point in the first "room" will arrest the eye and slow down progress before moving into the next space. Further focal points or details in the next "room" will give that space its own character.
4 A room or sitting space as small as 15 ft. wide by 10 ft. long could house two opposite benches tucked into the shrubs. Placing benches in this way opens up the width of a narrow plot (see also planting plan).

5 Hiding essentials such as the shed can be a problem in a long, narrow town garden where the whole design is viewed regularly from upstairs windows. The solution may be to site the shed neatly against the house wall to the side of the patio doors, where it will be less visible from upstairs windows than if it were placed at the far end of the garden.
6 The sunniest part of this garden is at the far end, so the last "room" opens out on to a bright, spacious patio. The strong pattern created by brick paving laid in a diagonal bond gives the impression of greater width.

Maximum privacy is afforded underneath the overhead beams in this town house garden. This westerly aspect catches the evening sun, while a facing bench takes advantage of the morning sun. The scent of the climbing shrubs is most pungent on summer evenings (*A*).

From the left: *Asplenium scolopendrium* 'Crispum' and *Hedera helix helix* 'Heise,' *Dryopteris wallichiana*, *Miscanthus sinensis* var. *purpurascens*, *Rosa* 'Parade,' *Lonicera japonica* 'Halliana,' *Hedera helix helix* 'Heise' and *Phlox paniculata* 'Blue Ice,' *Helianthemum* 'Cerise Queen.'

Two-tier planting makes full use of the space in this garden. The evergreen cotton lavender (*Santolina chamaecyparissus*) forms a permanent low-level backdrop to the container planted with bedding. In winter, the display might be replaced by pale pink winter-flowering heathers (*Erica carnea* 'Springwood Pink') and the salvias behind with the double early deep pink tulip 'Electra' (*B*).

From the left: *Philadelphus* 'Belle Etoile,' *Salvia × sylvestris* 'May Night,' *Lavandula angustifolia* 'Hidcote,' *Hemerocallis*; in the urn: *Cordyline australis* 'Purpurea,' *Diascia megathura*, *Verbena* 'Sissinghurst,' *Veronica gentianoides* 'Variegata,' *Helichrysum petiolare*; around the urn: *Santolina chamaecyparissus* var. *nana*.

The square or rectangular garden

A square is intrinsically static and in a very small garden it is difficult to add dramatic movement while keeping a balance between voids—by which I mean a patio, a lawn or a body of still water—and mass, which might include garden buildings and structures as well as plants, all of which give height. But some sense of movement can be created by encouraging the eye to move from one space or focal point to another, by using a design based on curves. However small the garden, it is good to create a distinct route through it, such as stepping stones through planting or grass. The character of the planting may then vary slightly and a subtle yet stunning plant could create a focal point en route.

A square plot may also have no view and one solution is to enhance the sense of enclosure, creating a tranquil private oasis. You do not need to keep to the square shape, but can introduce, say, a circle of lawn or paving in the center and surround it by lush planting. If the paving has a strong ground pattern it will act as an inward-pulling focus, especially when complemented by "architectural" planting. A very small square often lends itself to a static formal design, such as a geometric herb garden: low clipped hedges, brick paths, repeating planting and formal ornament are appropriate with a traditional house.

A rectangular plot which is roughly in the proportion of half width to length will have more inherent movement than a complete square. The design for a rectangle can use techniques described for long and narrow (see page 30) or square gardens. This shape lends itself to family living because it can easily be divided into two or three spaces. Three rooms, carefully linked, will give maximum space for everyday use and completely camouflage the shape of the plot. Pivoting the design on the diagonal gives the impression of a longer, wider garden. Diagonal lines have a strong sideways pull and exploit the maximum width to give a feeling of openness.

This roughly square garden, surrounded by fences, measures 31 ft. long by 23 ft. wide near the house and 27 ft. wide at the far end.

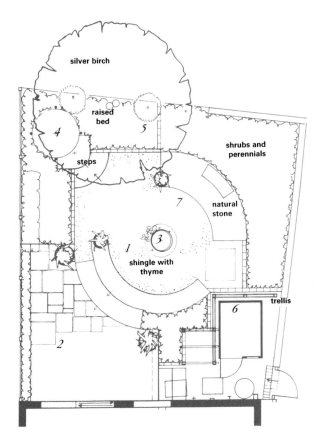

1 The curvaceous design flows around the central space, creating a sense of movement. It incorporates a slight change of level, with wide, shallow steps; by encouraging slower movement through the space, a more relaxed feel is achieved.

2 The patio doors of the house open onto a stone-paved area large enough for a table and four chairs, and backed by a narrow border. The microclimate here means that at times this patio can be too hot for sitting in.

3 A central water feature surrounded by cobblestones serves as a focal point and pulls the eye inward, reinforcing the sense of an enclosed oasis.

4 Steps lead up to a herringbone brick-paved patio which catches the evening sun but is otherwise shaded by the birch tree. A delicate, wrought-iron cupola supported on four pillars creates a small feature.

5 This garden is on a slope, the left-hand extremity being 1½ ft. higher than the right. The raised beds created on the left and on the far boundary are held back by brick retaining walls and help to balance the height of the house.

6 The sunken shed and bin storage area are camouflaged by a trellis screened by climbers trained over it.

7 A less defined paved surface such as gravel blends into its surrounds, and the informal planting growing in the gravel and spilling over the edges of the beds creates a soft, tranquil feel.

The brick path swings around an oval lawn in the central "room" of this garden. The curves help to counterbalance the straight outline of a rectangular plot. *Rosa* 'Compassion' and the evergreen ivy are supported by the trellis panel which completely screens the garden shed; evergreen foliage will ensure winter structure when these summer flowers are over.

Front, from the left: *Santolina chamaecyparissus,* *Choisya ternata,* *Weigela florida* 'Aureovariegata,' *Salvia* 'Rose Queen,' *Hebe* 'Midsummer Beauty,' *Campanula portenschlagiana.* On the fence, from the left: *Lonicera japonica* 'Halliana,' *Ilex aquifolium* 'Argenteomarginata,' *Hedera colchica* 'Dentata Variegata,' *Rosa* 'Compassion.'

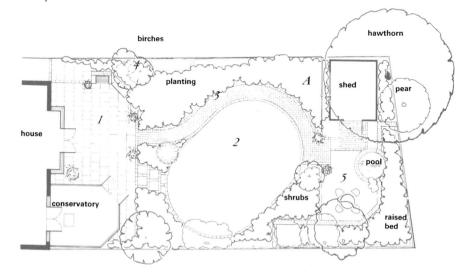

This garden, 54 ft. long by 30 ft. wide, is designed for family living. The area marked

A is shown with its planting scheme above, in summer.

1 A patio adjacent to the house, complete with barbecue, table and seat, gives ample space for outdoor entertaining. The lawn abutting the patio is separated from it by low planting.

2 An oval, brick-edged lawn, designed as a play area, lies diagonally across the center of the garden to give a sense of openness.

3 The strong directional flow of the brick path around the curved side of the lawn leads the eye on to the far "room."

4 A group of three birches, *Betula pendula* 'Dalecarlica,' *B. pendula* 'Purpurea' and *B. jacquemontii,* planted at 2 ft. intervals to keep them relatively small, forms a soft backdrop to the barbecue area, in addition to hiding neighboring properties viewed when looking back toward the house.

5 A smaller paved area at the far end of the garden, backed by a raised bed, catches the evening sun. An ornamental pool gives it a focal point.

33

The short, wide garden

A garden with little space lengthways from the house to the far boundary, but that is very wide from side to side, gives a foreshortened view and the design should aim to draw the eye to the side boundaries to lose the constricted feeling. A narrow bed, with dense, soft planting against the fence or wall in front of the view, will screen the physical barrier and help to alleviate the foreshortening.

It is important to select predominantly evergreen plants which do not have strong shapes, and very tall plants directly in front of the view should be avoided, as they will overpower and visually diminish the space. Flower colors should be soft (blues are particularly good), to accentuate the sense of distance. By fan-training shrubs on to the boundary fence or wall you will utilize minimum space for growing. A low-level focal point, such as a birdbath, will entice the viewer to look down, while the placing of a focal point at one extremity will encourage the eye to wander sideways.

If you are lucky enough to have a small plot with a lovely view, then all foreshortening problems can be solved by arranging the design and planting to take the eye beyond the boundary and bring the view into the garden. Arches are a successful way of framing views or garden features.

This country garden, surrounded by natural stone walls, is 56 ft. wide and its maximum length is only 15 ft. Planting schemes for the pool and the corner of the garden (2) are shown opposite, in summer.

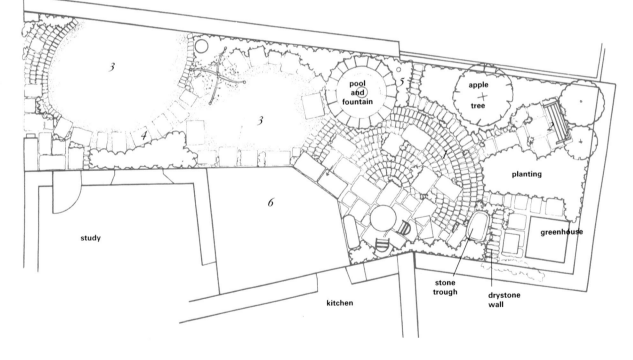

1 The patio's semi-circular shape and the direction in which the cobblestones are laid opens up the center space and leads the eye to the far corner of the garden.
2 The seat strategically placed in the corner acts as a focal point, encouraging the eye to wander sideways. The path leading to it from the patio reinforces this visual progression. The seat itself is partially screened by shrubs such as viburnum and berberis so that the boundary is half-concealed.

3 The two curved areas of lawn act as "voids" to help open up the tight space in the shortest part of the garden, where it is only 10 ft. from the house to the boundary.

4 The path, of flagstones set in grass, winds from the patio to the arbor and back around the other lawn, to make the most of the restricted length. The flagstones and the granite cobblestones, used around the arbor and one side of the far lawn, echo the materials of the patio.
5 The height of the rose (*Rosa* 'New Dawn') on a pillar blocks the view from neighboring windows.
6 The conservatory, planned at the same time as the garden, has an angled front designed to focus the view out to the fountain and pool.

A bench, diagonally placed in the corner of this short, squat garden, catches the evening sun and the view from it maximizes the width of the plot from side to side. When seen from the house, the bench acts as a focal point, again utilizing this width.

Clockwise from the left: *Sisyrinchium striatum*, *Dicentra exima*, *Paeonia lactiflora* 'Sarah Bernhardt,' *Viburnum × bodnantense* 'Dawn' with *Clematis* 'Bees' Jubilee,' *Berberis thunbergii* 'Rose Glow,' *Lavatera* 'Barnsley,' *Lavandula stoechas*, *Penstemon rostriflorus* 'Ruby,' *Hebe* 'Great Orme,' *Sisyrinchium striatum*.

The ground-level pool, with its central figure, draws the eye down and away from the near boundary wall (only 10 feet away from the house and conservatory). The soft, informal planting lends itself to a garden constructed in natural local stone.

Clockwise from the front: *Thymus × citriodorus* 'Bertram Anderson,' *Polystichum setiferum*, *Foeniculum vulgare* 'Bronze,' *Geum rivale*, *Hosta undulata* var. *undulata*, *P. setiferum*, *Bergenia* 'Abendglut,' *Hedera cristata*, *Rosa* 'New Dawn', *Acer palmatum* 'Dissectum Atropurpureum,' *B.* 'Abendglut,' *T. × citriodorus* 'Silver Posie'; in the pool: *Iris pseudacorus* 'Variegata.'

POSSIBILITIES OF THE SMALL GARDEN

The choice of materials that is now available for constructing and embellishing the small garden, as well as the range of possible styles, are as wide and varied as they are for larger plots. The key is to keep everything in balance with each other and in scale with the house and the overall space. Both formal and informal layouts and styles of planting can be appropriate, provided that there is a coherent, harmonious design. In an extremely small space the surfaces and boundaries themselves may in fact become a feature of the garden, where they are particularly prominent or have a strong design.

The choice of materials for this tiny town garden contributes to its harmonious design and meets its practical requirements. Trellis on the wall provides additional privacy and the arbor gives dappled shade over the seat. The paved surface allows dry access through the garden in all seasons. Predominantly evergreen shrubs, including Choisya ternata 'Sundance,' holly, fig and box, and climbers form a pleasing backdrop to these summer flowers.

A question of style

**PLANTING FOR A
SUNNY COURTYARD**

Acanthus

Choisya ternata

Cistus

Drimys winteri

Eucalyptus

Jasminum polyanthum

Lavandula

Olearia stellulata

Pittosporum tobira

Rosmarinus officinalis

*Santolina
    chamaecyparissus*

Solanum jasminoides
    'Album'

Yucca

Zantedeschia aethiopica

**NEAT-GROWING
SHRUBS FOR A
FORMAL GARDEN**

Buxus sempervirens

Choisya ternata
    'Sundance'

Hebe albicans 'Red Edge'

H. ochracea
    'James Stirling'

H. odora

Lonicera nitida

Pyracantha species

Rhododendron (azaleas)

*Rhododendron
    yakushimanum*
    and its hybrids

Skimmia japonica
    'Rubella'

Viburnum davidii

V. plicatum 'Mariesii'

The style of your garden will be largely created by the materials used and the selection of the individual plants. It is important that the style suits your particular garden setting, as well as meeting the practical dictates of the site and matching your own requirements and way of life. Not only should your choice of materials respect local building styles, but the plants should suit local growing conditions as well as the type of soil (see page 16).

Where a joint decision is involved, it is essential to agree upon the style before starting. So often one person prefers formality and the other informality. One solution is to create a fairly structured formal design and to introduce softness with the planting. Low clipped hedges surrounding a loose planting of perennials and a few shrubs not only gives the garden good winter structure and summer color but provides an attractive compromise between hard formality and total informality. This blend looks perfectly acceptable in most properties, new or old.

In many gardens, there is no clear-cut style or period to focus upon or to use as a starting point and therefore no limitations to the design. In new housing developments the whole plot can be featureless, without even a tree. Here you can develop your own style, in keeping with your furnishings and the house structure. You could match the boundary and paving materials to one of those used in the house, or the color scheme for a planting area near the house might reflect that of your main living space.

As a starting point, you might begin to appreciate and assess different styles by looking at private, national or historic gardens. Unfortunately not many small gardens are open to the public, but enclosed areas within larger gardens will help you to glean ideas. It is not necessary to work to a style with a specific title or label. However, rather like planning the decorating and furnishing of a room, the style must impose a unity on the garden in order to give a pleasing design which works well in its surroundings. There are many stylistic influences from the past, as widely differing as the symmetrical designs that characterized large, formal period gardens and the billowing informality that epitomized cottage gardens in the rural tradition. The essence of these distinct styles can be distilled and utilized successfully in today's small gardens.

The influence of overseas garden design has introduced new styles and ideas to our repertoire. Many of the elements of Japanese gardens, for example, are appropriate in small spaces and they generally require low maintenance. A gravel surface would replace the lawn, planting is fairly sparse, and the inclusion of water would add movement and life to the calm, static set. Many of the plants most fitting to a Japanese style of garden have bold or architectural forms; some, such as *Cornus controversa* or cultivars and hybrids of *Acer palmatum*, offer an attractive branched pattern. Appropriate evergreens provide year-round backdrop and structure: bamboos, camellias, osmanthus, kalmias, photinias as well as bay and dwarf or topiary pines are all suitable in a small space. Spring- or early-summer-flowering deciduous shrubs and trees counterpoint the evergreens and provide seasonal interest: *Prunus, Chaenomeles, Enkianthus, Syringa, Hydrangea, Viburnum, Forsythia* and *Spiraea* are all appropriate.

ABOVE LEFT *In this Japanese-style garden, appropriate plants— bamboos, ivies, ferns and a vine—enclose the space, while stones of different sizes create an interesting pattern on the loose cobblestone surface.*

ABOVE *The Persian theme of this garden creates a strong, formal design. Clipped dwarf box hedges enclose the beds,* Minuartia verna *emphasizes the curved brick step in the foreground and matching plantings of* Lonicera nitida *'Baggesen's Gold' and* Euonymus fortunei *'Emerald 'n Gold' fill the far beds.*

A small, enclosed, sunny courtyard gives ample scope for creating a garden with a Moorish character. The warmth reflected from the walls creates a sheltered microclimate which is more protected, especially in winter, enabling the use of plants usually grown in a Mediterranean climate. In emulating the style of a Persian or Moorish garden, the lush plants might be balanced with a watercourse running through a paved area: a combination of warm terra-cotta tiles and pebbles gives an exotic feel. The sun-filled garden would radiate heat, which might be enhanced by the use of bold flower colors and evergreen foliage (see the list, left).

The formal garden

The purely formal style is symmetrical, so that the design provides mirror images. Straight lines, balustrades, statuary, formal pools, vistas and clipped hedges all epitomize formality. The overall look is neat and tidy, with regular outlines and the planting contained within a designated area.

The word "vista" conjures up pictures of rolling acres but vistas in lesser proportion can help to increase the feeling of space in a small area. A tiny enclosed courtyard might have a *trompe l'oeil* expansive country scene painted on the far wall, framed by some formal ivy-clad trelliswork. Less dramatic are vistas created by reflecting small scenes in a mirror, thus giving the impression that they carry on or are repeated down the length of the garden. A narrow rectangular pool, occupying the length of the garden, could be reflected in a mirror mounted on the far wall.

Selecting appropriate materials for the surfaces and boundaries will reinforce a formal design at the same time as linking the house with the garden. Square or rectangular paving slabs in most materials are suitable, provided they are laid in a set pattern; bricks work extremely well in a formal setting, the patterns created by the bonding giving precise shapes; gravel looks equally appropriate in a formal or informal setting, depending on how it is used (see page 44). An existing dull fence boundary can be improved by fixing trellis panels of a formal design in front, and fan-training shrubs such as pyracanthas against it. The clean-cut lines of dressed natural stone walls, neatly jointed and pointed, have a classical feel yet fit well into the rural or urban environs around small formal gardens.

To complete the formality, it is essential that you include some plants which have a strong architectural shape and are easy to keep tidy or which grow naturally in a neat shape (see the list, left). Repeated plantings provide cohesion in any design but symmetrical placing becomes even more important in a formal layout. A central lawn or patio may be enclosed by matching borders on either side; repeat groups of plants in the borders will reinforce the balance and continuity. A low, clipped hedge around a bed will maintain formal precision when a softer, more loose planting scheme is enclosed within. Low hedges also provide invaluable winter structure in the garden. Topiary shapes are the essence of formal planting design, whether their precise form is spherical, conical or cuboid, and whether grown as a low bush or as a standard on a stem.

The informal garden

Informal gardens need structure and unity but, rather than being strictly symmetrical, they achieve balance through the careful juxtaposition of their features. Informal shapes are usually irregular, often flowing and with more random patterns predominating. The edges of a patio can be less precisely defined and gravel or planting may be allowed to merge into paving slabs or a path laid in brick.

A rectangular or square urban plot may be softened by the use of curves and a flowing design. Curves should always be bold and positive; a curve must go somewhere, either to lead the eye to a focal point or to link the shapes you have created in your garden design, whether it be an area of lawn, a planting bed or a patio. A winding path in a small garden is best paved with small units, such as bricks, granite cobblestones or gravel, to avoid numerous costly cuts and unsightly joints which break up the flow of the route. Bricks, pavers and granite cobblestones are small enough to create curved edges, even where larger paving slabs have been used.

Picket and palisade fences both have an informal feel and provide a low, open boundary suitable for a rural or urban front garden. Natural stone walls are well suited to rural gardens, where they blend with the local materials and surroundings. Haphazard planting as well as self-seeding into the crevices of a dry stone wall add charm and variety to the informal nature of a design.

Informality in an urban space, however small, can be expressed by extensive planting on the boundaries, using tall growing shrubs such as *Photinia × fraseri* 'Birmingham,' *Amelanchier canadensis* and *Ilex aquifolium* cultivars, as well as additional planting of ground cover, for example *Ajuga reptans*, *Cotoneaster microphyllus* and *Viola tricolor*. The use of large-leaved shrubs in the foreground, adjacent to the house, with smaller-leaved shrubs and perennials further away and on either side of a narrow, winding informal path, will have the effect of losing the clearly defined depth of the garden. Lush planting will bring informality to any urban garden; for example a vine-clad arch leading to the patio softens the entry and adds a welcome feeling of seclusion.

PLANTS FOR
MODERN LINES
Cordyline australis
Festuca glauca 'Blauglut'
Hedera helix helix
Ilex aquifolium
  'Pyramidalis'
Juniperus × media
  'Gold Coast'
Mahonia × media 'Charity'
Miscanthus sinensis
  'Zebrinus'
Phormium 'Dazzler'
Pinus mugo 'Mops'
Rheum 'Ace of Hearts'
Sasa veitchii
Sinarundinaria nitida
Thamnocalamus
  spathaceus
Vinca minor
Yucca

PLANTS FOR
INFORMAL GARDENS
Berberis thunbergii
  'Rose Glow'
Dianthus 'Doris'
D. 'Mrs Sinkins'
Digitalis
Eranthis hyemalis
Geranium
  'Johnson's Blue'
Hosta
Lavandula
Narcissus (small growing
  species and cultivars)
Perovskia 'Blue Spire'
Philadelphus
  'Manteau d'Hermine'
Spiraea japonica
  'Gold Flame'

LEFT *The use of bricks bedded in sand makes an appropriate surface in an informal garden. Thyme growing in the paving and Saponaria ocymoides, Nepeta, Vinca minor and Sedum spectabile tumbling over the walls, enhance the informality.*

RIGHT *The use of man-made materials transform this roof into a modern outdoor living room. The metal trellis provides a windbreak, protecting the Juniperus horizontalis and other plants. Container-grown grasses are tolerant of exposed situations and of pollution.*

The modern garden

A small enclosed space with no particular style to integrate provides the possibility of adopting a modern approach to garden design. You can experiment with man-made and less traditional materials. Plants are used in a more contrived, less naturalistic way; chosen for their strong shape or form, they are planted in bold groups to make a strong statement rather than a soft association.

Metal, concrete, slate, marble, glass, mosaics, tiles and wood all provide exciting design materials and reflect the construction of a modern house besides coordinating well with a contemporary interior. The patio, for example, can be surfaced with a metal weldmesh-style grid and its design echoed in metal trellis panels used to enclose the space. These can be made to your design by a blacksmith or metal specialist and you may be able to assemble the pieces on site yourself. However, it would be necessary to obtain expert advice to make sure the metal was properly treated and securely fixed for outdoor use. The cost would vary enormously, depending on the metal used and how it was treated; stainless steel would be very expensive.

Water can be channeled through clear acrylic chutes into a stainless-steel reservoir in which colored glass marbles take the place of cobblestones. Other ways of introducing water into a modern design might include the use of linked glazed ceramic bowls, copper wall-mounted water features or a fountain made of shiny stainless-steel tubes. For any of these ideas, you would need to find a craftsperson specializing in working with acrylic or stainless steel, perhaps through a garden contractor.

Minimal planting with a limited range of species of distinct form or character (see the list, left) can be set either into the ground or in containers designed as an integral part of the construction. Grasses, phormiums, yuccas and plants with strong architectural shapes enhance a modern design and their sculptural lines have a dramatic impact in a small garden. Another creative approach is to work around a theme and interpret this in a modern, stylized way. A good example is a sun and moon garden in which a grass circle edged with light-colored bricks repre-

sents the sun, while a darker material is used to pave a crescent-shaped patio. The color schemes move from dark to light: the plants in the moon garden are dark greens with dusky flower colors, blending with gray and silver foliage; the sun garden has lighter greens and bright flower colors (see the lists, right).

Colored rubberized surfaces, often used in playgrounds, provide a bright alternative to traditional paving materials and edging treatments such as brick will link this modern material to a house. They can be laid on a stable existing base or patio and are very suitable in a garden for young children.

Concrete walls have a suitably contemporary neutral appearance; they can be painted white or a color of your choice to provide an attractive backdrop. This would combine well with the interesting textures and finishes made possible with the use of concrete and aggregate paving slabs. Hexagonal paving or small squares inserted between octagons can be used to create a ground pattern that reflects the design of an adjacent kitchen or perhaps a conservatory floor.

PLANTS FOR A SUN AND MOON GARDEN

FOLIAGE AND FLOWERS IN DARK SHADES
Cimicifuga simplex
  'Brunette'
Garrya elliptica
Geranium phaeum
Liriope muscari
Mahonia aquifolium
Ophiopogon planiscapus
  'Nigrescens'
Osmanthus delavayi
Rosa glauca
Taxus baccata 'Fastigiata'

SILVER FOLIAGE
Anthemis punctata
  cupaniana
Artemisia 'Powis Castle'
Brachyglottis 'Sunshine'
Eryngium × zabelii
  'Violetta'
Phormium tenax
  'Variegatum'
Pyrus salicifolia 'Pendula'

FOLIAGE AND FLOWERS IN YELLOW AND GOLD
Acer shirasawanum
  aureum
Achillea 'Moonshine'
Choisya ternata
  'Sundance'
Clematis tangutica
Coreopsis verticillata
  'Moonbeam'
Narcissus yellow-flowered
  species
Taxus baccata 'Aurea'

Garden surfaces

Gravel, grass and concrete paving are successfully blended in this small town garden. Each "room" has its own character, readily identified by the use of different surfacing materials, but continuity is provided too; the brick raised bed in the far corner reflects the brick risers of the steps in the next space. Plants in containers, including petunias, fuchsia and agapanthus, soften the look of the steps.

In a small garden the pressures on space tend to be far greater than they are in a larger garden and the surfaces must reflect this degree of use. For example, because the lawn area is less in a small garden it will be put under greater stress, possibly making grass not the most practical choice. Paved surfaces are generally far more practical than soft surfaces, allowing year-round use without any damage. As one of the main components in the small space, the hard surface is on view continually and will need to be durable, level, easy to sweep clean and well drained, drying out quickly after rain, as well as complementing the house and its surroundings.

Where space is very restricted and yet regularly used, a fully paved garden with planting pockets might be considered the most practical solution. The paved backdrop can be relatively insignificant, with other features providing the interest or focal points. Variation in texture can be created by combining materials, such as using brick detailing in concrete-slab paving, or by mulching planted areas with gravel (see page 44). There is a wide range of suitable paving materials for a small garden and teaming one or two together can create pleasing effects. For instance, natural flagstones can be set off by inset bricks which may link the design to a garden structure, such as the brick piers of a pergola. Most paving materials are equally suitable for a front garden and will be strong enough for the weight of a car, provided you lay a deep enough sub-base. In general the minimum depth should be 3 in., but allow at least twice that depth for cars. Foundation depths will also vary according to underlying ground materials; a specification must be prepared for each site.

Algae growth is a common problem in enclosed areas where shade predominates and a lack of air circulation will slow down the drying out of the paving. If your garden is in shade, lay the paving with a good fall ($\frac{1}{2}$ in. in 3 ft.) away from the house for maximum drainage and avoid using riven or textured slabs which harbor pockets of moisture. A degree of weathering can look attractive but excessive greening will make the surface slippery and dangerous. Regular cleaning with a brand-name fluid will remove algal growth.

Bricks, tiles and clay pavers

Paving in small units is both extremely versatile and visually in keeping with the scale of the smaller garden. To achieve unity, choose a material that matches that of the house or the garden boundaries. Whether you are constructing a path, a patio or a flight of steps, multiples of small units will create interesting patterns and allow turns and curves to be more easily constructed. Full-sized bricks laid side to side on edge can create a curve on a radius of about $4\frac{1}{2}$ ft. without you having to make any cuts. Half-bricks laid on edge will make a curve on a radius of about 2 ft. 4 in. Bricks can be cut, using a club hammer and a cold chisel, but you should always use full bricks on perimeters (on a concrete footing) where stability is required.

RIGHT *Bricks can be laid flat (frog down, as here), on edge or on end, each producing a different look; they are ideal for creating a curved path. An herb bed in the paving contains rosemary, lavender, thyme and chives, all of which thrive in a sunny situation.*

BELOW RIGHT *Terra-cotta tiles can be used for garden paving provided they are frost-resistant. The colors of these tiles have softened with age to create a pleasing backdrop to the informal planting.*

sophisticated garden. Square or rectangular tiles are most apt in a small garden, as many-sided shapes make the surface look too busy. They vary in price, natural stone tiles being the most expensive, but the cheapest will equate to the better-quality bricks.

I recommend laying bricks and tiles on a continuous 1 in. wet mortar bed, with wet mortar pointed joints in between to provide a neat, low-maintenance finish. However, gaps in the pointing, perhaps filled with gravel, sand or soil, will soften the hard look of a patio and enable plants to be grown in the cracks, but more aftercare is required to keep weeds and moss under control, as they too will readily invade the open joints. Pavers can be laid on a sand bed and are best finished with a weak sand/cement mix brushed into the joints.

Clay pavers are now made to match bricks and are often seen in front gardens. The overall look is similar to brick but they can only be used for paving, not for walling. They are durable and frost-resistant and cost much the same as bricks, though many have a harder, more regular look.

The high temperatures reached during the manufacture of some clay tiles and frost-resistant bricks cause the impurities in the clay to burn away, giving pock marks and variations in color when they are fired. Each brick acquires its own tone and character, which brings individuality to brick surfaces in the garden. The patterns created by the way bricks are laid can be used to emphasize or detract from the garden's shape. Cross-bonding will foreshorten the view, for example, while bricks laid end to end in a running bond will accentuate the length of a path. Bonds such as basketweave and herringbone are static and well suited to a sitting-out area.

Terra-cotta floor tiles used as a paving surface may give the garden a Mediterranean or even a Mexican flavor. They must be frost-resistant and recommended by the manufacturer for outdoor use. Natural stone tiles, such as slate, have a natural beauty, with a wide variation in color, from greens to grays to browny pinks, and they add class to the

Viola tricolor

This lovely little wild flower, which we know as heartsease, will grow and seed itself in any nook or cranny. It was first named by the Anglo-Saxons "bonewort" and later took the more pleasing name "pansy" from the French pensées, meaning thoughts. The Elizabethan poets gave it several more names, including "pancyes," "hartes-ease," "love-in-idleness" and "Pinkeney John." Later popular names were "flame flower," "Herb Trinity" and "Johnny jump-ups."

Natural stone

With its natural variation in coloring and its weathering properties, stone undoubtedly has an inherent beauty and its mellow, natural appearance lends itself to use in the outdoor room. Large pieces of natural stone make an appropriate paving material however small the garden; its simplicity ensures that it never looks fussy or out of proportion. Do not be tempted to skimp if you really like the appearance of natural stone—although it is one of the most expensive materials, in a small garden you do not need a vast quantity and the amount you might save by buying a cheaper, imitation material is minimal compared to the overall expenditure. The cost of laying is marginally higher for natural stone of random thickness.

You should investigate local stone-based products first if your property and environs have a distinctive regional character. Harmony is important in a small space and buildings constructed in any natural materials will be complemented by paving, walling and other features made of natural stone. Whether newly quarried or reclaimed, random or rectangular, stone slabs, with their individual, generous proportions, can give a sense of space to a small patio and if they reflect the dimensions of a section of a window or door frame, this will provide continuity. Sawn natural stone is a beautiful, precise, but expensive material which looks equally appropriate in a formal or informal situation. Its versatility allows for continuity within the design, as it works well not only for paving but for walls, step treads and even seats and barbecue worktops. Its main disadvantage is that it becomes slippery when wet if algae have formed on the surface; this can be avoided by regular cleaning.

It is possible to cut stone to shape, or to fit a very small area, but this is costly and too many cuts lose the original effect. A smaller area of paving lends itself to broken pieces of stone laid in a random, informal pattern, known as irregular paving. This is all too often badly laid and looks clumsy and ugly, but it can be done skillfully: pieces must interlock to avoid large spaces and joints, otherwise the temptation is to fill them with excessive quantities of mortar. A flush joint, ½ in. wide at most, looks the most unobtrusive.

Slate and marble are expensive, but they have a crisp, precise look, well suited to continuity between indoor and outdoor use in the small formal or modern garden. Slate, particularly green slate, makes a neutral backdrop to planting and looks most attractive when wet. The thin, lightweight pieces of slate are ideal for roof gardens; although lightweight, they are not fragile provided they are laid properly, on a firm foundation; this would need to be specified by an architect or structural engineer in relation to your roof garden. Marble gives a more Mediterranean feel to an outdoor space and, used in moderation, enhances a sunny area. Regular cleaning is required to prevent it becoming slippery.

Gravel and cobblestones

Gravel looks appropriate in both formal and informal gardens, depending on how it is used. A well-laid brick edge containing a gravel area will enhance the precise look of a formal garden, whereas a wandering gravel path is more fitting in an informal design because its form is unstructured and irregular. Gravel (rounded) and stone chippings (angular) are less expensive to lay than a rigid surface. The same sub-base is used for gravel as for other paving (see page 42). The gravel itself is laid loose in a thin layer no deeper than 1 in. on top of a "binding layer" of fine dust which seals the coarse aggregate in the sub-base underneath.

RIGHT *Gravel forms a link between paved areas and is a low-maintenance medium in which to grow plants in pockets. Dig a hole through the gravel and sub-base to the soil below; after planting in the usual way, cover the top of the soil with a thin layer of gravel.*

BELOW LEFT *Natural stone makes a perfect foil for planted containers. The random, rectangular slabs should be laid with a ½-in. joint; try to avoid continuous lines. They may be wet mortar pointed for a permanently weed-free surface, or a sand/soil mix may be brushed in the joints and plants encouraged to grow in the gaps.*

Gravel is available in a wide range of colors, shapes and sizes of stone. The shades will vary in wet and dry weather—usually richer colors shine out when the gravel is damp. Its interesting textures and colors can brighten an area of the garden not regularly used, or a light well. The movement of gravel may be a problem in a small garden, being a temptation for small children to eat or throw and the smaller size of pea gravel collecting on shoes. Turning car wheels in a confined parking area will also move the gravel around continually and a fixed surface will wear far better. Always avoid gravel on a sloping site. To keep the surface clean it will need regular raking to remove debris; an occasional top-dressing of fresh gravel will be required to replace any gravel removed by wear and tear.

You could introduce larger, rounded cobblestones to vary the texture of the gravel. Cobblestones are smooth, rounded, generally water-washed and vary in size from ¾–4 in. They may be bedded in mortar (see below) to form a permanent paved surface. The uneven finish is uncomfortable to walk on, which makes it useful as a surface where one wishes to deter pedestrian traffic. As a detail in a patio or paved area, cobblestones add interest and texture but the surface will be unsuitable for tables and chairs. As a loose element they associate particularly well with water and single rocks in planting, creating an unusual feature.

Laying stone slabs

When laying regular paving, always use a higher proportion of larger to smaller pieces and bed it on a continuous mortar bed, on top of a sub-base (see page 42), spreading one area of mortar at a time. Start in the furthest corner of the patio or paved area and work out from there so you do not need to walk over completed work. Place individual stones to achieve a balanced mix of sizes over the whole area. Arrange the larger pieces around smaller keystones, trying to avoid joints running in straight lines.

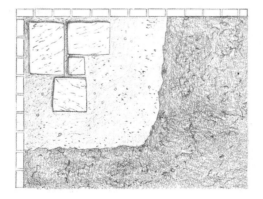

Start by placing a large stone in the furthest corner and work out from there.

Try to achieve a balance of different-sized stones over the whole area to be paved.

Concrete and reconstituted stone slabs

Reconstituted materials are generally cheaper than natural products and are more readily available but they have to be used with caution in a small garden. Older buildings in particular have a strong association with natural products and here man-made materials must be incorporated sympathetically. Some reproduction materials do not bear any resemblance to the original product and a bad match will jar in a confined space, but reproduction natural stone slabs, combined with the local gravel, can tie modern and old together. Some concrete paving slabs have no texture and tend to look rather dull, although some of the better-quality products (see below) will form a neutral, less expensive surface. Many concrete products are colored and, while it may seem a good idea to tie them in with furnishings in an adjacent room of the house, these artificial colors fade in time, defeating the original object.

The composition of reconstituted stone slabs is generally superior to that of concrete paving slabs because it is a mix of concrete and natural stone. But the presence of the aggregate (pieces of stone chippings or gravel, varying in color) in the reconstituted stone slabs makes them difficult to cut and yet retain a clean face. For shaping the tread of a curved step, for example, a much neater edge will be achieved by using natural stone sawn to size. Broken concrete paving, laid as irregular paving, might initially appear to be a cheap surface; but if laid properly, as previously described for broken stone, the time taken to lay it increases the cost in line with new paving slabs. Small-unit concrete blocks might be a better, and equally cheap, solution; they fit well with larger unit paving and some look quite natural, almost like granite cobblestones, having been tumbled during manufacture to soften the edges and look worn.

Timber and bark

Timber has many uses in the garden. Wooden deck gardens as shown in the photograph above, fit well into small spaces, creating an interesting feature and using the space efficiently. Decking enables a patio to be raised above ground level to enjoy the benefit of the sun, which is well worth considering in a small space surrounded by other houses. Building up over

an existing patio may be preferable to starting again if access is poor and the removal of debris is impractical. The relatively light weight of decking makes it ideal for roof gardens and the method of construction, with boards supported on rafters placed on permeable pads, allows water to flow underneath the roof to drain freely and prevents the timber rotting. Access below the boards is also relatively easy for maintenance purposes by lifting individual boards, as for floorboards. Kit forms are easy to construct and softwood treated with preservative will have a long lifespan and is less expensive than hardwood. A non-toxic preservative should be used so that plant growth is not affected and all cuts must be treated during assembly. Use galvanized metal or stainless-steel nails so that the wood does not stain. Timber surfaces can be very slippery in wet weather and regular cleaning will be needed.

Sawn log pieces are useful for creating stepping-stone paths in densely planted areas where tree roots may lift and crack paved surfaces or there is insufficient depth for paving footings. Bark chippings laid around the stepping stones extends the "paved" area and continues the rustic feel. A bark path mingles well into planting where no defined edge is required, creating an unobtrusive route which is ideal for leading to a storage or compost area.

Timber decking is laid on a series of support frames which in turn sit on a hardcore sub-base to ensure good drainage and a stable, level surface. Here the decking is laid to emphasize the length of this small space; narrow joints between the boards allow for expansion of the wood. Annual cleaning with a brand-name algicide will minimize the growth of algae, which make the surface slippery.

Lawns

RIGHT *A decorative, low-growing lawn is made from mind-your-own business* (Soleirolia solerolii); *it needs a moist soil to thrive.*

LAWN ALTERNATIVES

If you want a green area mainly to look out on, there are several attractive alternatives to grass. Chamomile is less hard-wearing than a regular lawn and will not tolerate children playing on it, but it forms a pleasing, rich green sight and needs less regular tending than grass. It should be planted in a sunny, well-drained site and will take a year to establish, during which time you must be prepared to weed in between the plants. Buy small plantlets and space them about 4 in. apart; *Chaemaemelum nobilis* 'Treneague' is the best to use for a lawn. Creeping thyme (*Thymus serpyllum* in all its varieties) is planted in the same way; it also needs a sunny site and well-drained soil.

A lawn is such a characteristic part of the English garden that many traditional designs include one, however restricted the size of the plot. The addition of a grassed area adds another dimension: the stretch of green has a restful quality. There will inevitably be drawbacks to having a lawn in a small garden, such as the heavy use it receives, the shade cast from neighboring trees, boundaries and buildings and the maintenance required to keep it looking good. But many people are prepared to contend with these for the pleasure of a grassed area.

Because the lawn will undoubtedly be small, it is imperative to create a simple shape, avoiding awkward corners which cannot easily be cut with a mower. Edging will need to be done weekly in the growing season to keep the garden tidy. To minimize this task, lay a brick or paved edge butting up to the grass area which will enable the mower to run over the surface and cut the edges. This edge must be laid on a concrete footing, or the roots will slowly move it. The shape of the lawn can be used as an integral part of the garden's design. For example, in a rectangular garden you could introduce a curved brick mowing edge; this would divide the lawn from the borders but at the same time increase the feeling of space (see page 33). If broad enough, the mowing edge can double as a path.

In a small space, not only is every bit of lawn likely to be well used, but extremes of heat or shade will cause stresses on the grass. Shade present for most of the day on one part of the lawn will encourage permanent dampness and therefore moss growth. Similarly, a daily sun-baked lawn will dry out and turn brown. Sowing the correct mix initially will give the lawn a good start but only long-term maintenance will keep moss at bay and produce a good-quality sward (see page 92).

Choosing the right grasses

In selecting the right grass seed or sod you must consider the aspect of the garden, the amount of sun/shade it receives, and the lawn's intended use. If you are laying sod, look at samples before purchase

and assess the proportion of coarse or fine grasses. The main varieties of grasses that are available today are broadly divided into top quality and utility grade grasses. Top-quality cool season lawn grasses have fine leaves and, when used alone, produce a high-quality lawn after proper ground preparation and the correct maintenance regime. These grasses are generally slower-growing, will not stand up to hard wear and must be cared for on a regular basis. They will tolerate close mowing. Utility-grade cool season grasses include perennial rye grass, bents and meadow grass. These are the tougher, coarser grass species, used in conjunction with the finer grasses for a thick, closely knit turf. They will not stand close mowing. Perennial rye grass is hard-wearing, fast-growing, tolerates heavy soil and is hardy in winter.

For heavy use, including play, the lawn sod or seed mix will need to contain about 40 percent rye grass with 55 percent fescue and 5 percent bent. A lawn which will take some traffic should have 25 percent meadow grass, 65 percent fescue and 10 percent bent. In warm climates traditional grasses include Bermuda, St. Augustine and Zoysia. These particular grasses are known as warm season grasses, and they are most usually grown as single-species lawns.

Laying a lawn

However good the grass mix, the success of your lawn will also depend on the thoroughness of your ground preparation. If you move into a new house, the sodded plot you acquire may be little more than subsoil badly compacted by builders' heavy machinery with about 2 in., if you are lucky, of topsoil and some badly laid field sod on top. If you feel that this is not a good time to start splashing out and spending a lot of money, the answer is to try a rigorous maintenance program and improve what you have, at least as a temporary measure. But if the original grass quality is at fault this will be a false economy and you will eventually have to give it up and start again.

If you wish to sow or lay a new lawn from scratch, you will need to remove all builder's rubble and rubbish from the area before cultivating it to one and a half to two spades' depth, at the same time incorporating some well-rotted organic matter (see page 88) and gritty material if you need to improve the drainage. If you have only a thin covering of topsoil, you will have to import some more, to a depth of at least 6 in. You must get rid of all perennial weeds, such as quack grass. Finally, firm the ground and level it well to ensure that the mower does not scalp any high patches or leave long grass in the depressions.

Sod or seed?

The decision about whether to lay sod or sow seed will depend on several factors. Sod is more expensive but in a small space it may be worth spending a little more for an instant visual effect, although you need to allow six weeks before walking on newly laid sod. Sod is normally laid in the spring, and it should ideally be laid the day you buy it and a spell of dry weather following laying can cause cracks to appear unless you water it vigilantly. Although it is easy to achieve neat, well-defined edges to a sodded lawn, laying it to a good standard overall is more difficult than sowing a lawn.

Sowing a lawn from seed (see below) is cheaper and easier, although the preparation of a level, weed-free seedbed is time-consuming. A seeded lawn takes longer to establish as the seeds first have to germinate, then grow and spread to cover the ground—a spring-sown lawn is not usable until late summer. You must eliminate all weed seedlings to prevent them from competing with the grass seed for light, water and food, and must keep cats and birds off the lawn while it is establishing. Spring and early fall are the only times when a lawn can be seeded, preferably when the weather is warm enough for growth but neither too wet nor too dry. If you want a lawn to suit particular requirements, then a seed mixture is the only choice, as sod rarely comes in anything other than a standard form.

Sowing a lawn

When the prepared soil is fairly dry, rake any lumps into fine particles. Firm the soil by light treading or using the rake head. Rake the soil level, remove any stones or debris, then firm again. If no organic matter has been incorporated, apply a pre-seeding fertilizer and rake it in 7–10 days before sowing. Sow half the seed by traversing the plot in one direction, scattering it in a broadcast fashion, then scatter the remaining half by walking across the site at right angles. After sowing, lightly rake over the seedbed.

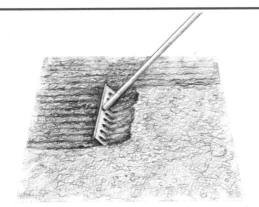

Rake and firm the soil several times until the seedbed is completely level and firm, but not compacted; tamp down all soft spots.

For even sowing, mark out the site into regular divisions; follow the manufacturer's instructions about quantities.

Boundaries

There are many possibilities for boundary treatments, as shown in this terrace, and each should respect the design of the neighboring garden as well as your own. Simply painting a wall or standard woven fence panel white makes a mundane boundary more attractive, provided it is in keeping with the overall style of the garden. Trellis placed on top of a wall gives extra privacy.

The boundaries of a small garden need special care. A discrete boundary, such as a low wall, or an open boundary will bring the view beyond into your garden and increase the feeling of space. In a site adjoining other small gardens, an open fence, such as post and rail, is simple and inexpensive to construct. Or a wrought-iron fence will denote an urban boundary without being overpowering in a small space. Shared boundaries or those viewed by passers-by must be at one with the neighborhood. In a confined space it is unwise to antagonize the neighbors by dealing with joint boundaries unsympathetically. The material selected should echo some element of the fabric of the house to give a unifying effect. It must also be chosen for its practical contribution, considering the cost, durability, lon-

gevity and level of maintenance—do not be tempted to use a poor substitute because it is cheap. The boundary may need to be dog- or child-proof or to offer a degree of privacy, in which case you will choose a solid boundary such as a wall or close-boarded fence; on the other hand planning regulations may require it to be open plan. Selection of the appropriate materials will enhance the periphery of your property, providing a means of vertical gardening and not a permanent eyesore surrounding your space.

Walls

Walls emphasize the feeling of enclosure and can be constructed in brick, natural stone or concrete materials. As a natural stone look-alike, concrete is not very effective and should be avoided, but the light-reflecting properties of a white-painted concrete block or rendered wall can be invaluable in a dark basement or a very enclosed garden. Paint colors can even be selected to match interior furnishing, but remember that painted walls require frequent maintenance so you should support climbers on wooden or plastic trellis, fixed to the wall with hooks, to facilitate access (see page 98). Walls cost more to construct than most other boundaries, brick perhaps costing twice as much as a concrete construction and many times more than a ready-made fence. Maintenance is minimal and longevity is assured, however. With natural weathering, walls become more attractive as time passes. To ensure permanence, they must be built on an adequate concrete base: the higher the wall the wider and deeper the footing should be. A boundary wall 5 to 6 ft. high will give privacy within the garden, without casting too much shade. For any wall over 3 ft. high you should seek professional advice on footing specification and the actual construction of the wall.

A boundary or indeed an internal wall may need to retain earth as part of its function. The construction must be even more robust to hold the weight and expert advice will be essential. If you are not building the wall yourself, always check that the reverse of solid concrete and brick retaining walls has been waterproofed, that weepholes have been included for drainage and there is an open-textured backfill, such as gravel, immediately behind for drainage. Low retaining walls (15 to 18 in. high) form ideal seating and are useful where there is a limited patio area. Wider coping stones or a wooden top or even decorative cushions make a more comfortable seat and strengthen the inside-out concept.

In an enclosed garden, it is likely that at least one boundary will not belong to you; this may be a fence or a neighbor's house or garage wall. They are often unsightly and may need camouflaging with plants; always seek permission before fixing climbing supports to a neighbor's structure.

Brick

Brick is an ideal material for both urban and rural areas where brick buildings predominate. Because it is made from a natural product, clay, the variation in color is soft and blends easily with other natural materials and plants. Engineering bricks have a smooth, shiny finish and are best suited to a modern garden. Stock bricks have a rougher, less precise finish and some are even slightly twisted due to the high temperature in the center of the kiln during firing. These are a bricklayer's dread but I find them particularly attractive—they give the wall a rustic feel, most apt for an older property. Always check that fired-clay bricks are classified as frost-resistant quality, which means they will be durable even when saturated and subjected to repeated freezing and thawing. There is little risk of frost attack in engineering (calcium silicate) bricks.

A damp-proof course at both top and bottom of the wall is recommended to prevent the penetration of rainwater and ground moisture. Wall copings protect the brickwork from rain and selecting paving slabs, tiles or slate for this can link the design with materials used in a path or patio. Efflorescence or white deposits on the face of new brickwork is not a serious problem and will weather away. Honeycomb brick walls provide a good screen. Their open construction makes them less dominant and, besides being cheaper to build, they make ideal plant supports.

Stone

This is a very durable material, with a wide range of color variation from area to area. There are many methods of construction and finishes, from coursed dry stone walls, flint walls, random mortared rubble walls, quarry-finished dressed stone walls to reconstituted stone walls. Provided they are not too high, stone walls, with their natural coloring, will not be overpowering. A dry stone wall with planting pockets can extend the growing area in a small garden. The exact lines of dressed stone (sawn or polished after quarrying) are suitable for a garden in a modern design or in an urban area. Quarried stone can also be cut for paving to match the walling.

Clematis florida 'Sieboldii' and Actinidia kolomikta *make a pleasing composition against the brick wall; they are ideal plants for a narrow space where forward growth must be minimized. Select clematis as companion plants which require pruning at the same time as their host, so they can be cut back together.*

Fences

Being relatively cheap, fences are the most commonly used form of boundary. They are perfectly suitable for a small garden and fence construction is a task far more people will be happy to undertake themselves than building a wall. Fences are usually bought in panels, which are fixed to posts set at 6 to 9 ft. intervals at the most, and firmly fixed in the ground by concreting or a brand-name fixing system. Concrete posts have the longest life but look very ugly initially, although in time they weather down and become softened with planting. Ownership of a fence is usually determined by having the "back" with the arris or supporting rails in your garden, and this means you will be responsible for repair or replacement. If a neighbor's fence is in poor condition, erect a panel or panels of trellis on your side, adjacent to the fence, to ensure that the plant support does not blow down in a gale.

The more robust the timber and the better the method of fixing, the longer the potential life of the fence. Select timber that has been preservative-impregnated by a vacuum process, because untreated softwood will have a very limited life. The off-the-peg styles of close-board, feather board and woven fences, bought as standard-size panels, all provide privacy but are not especially attractive and some can be very flimsy. With a little imagination and small extra cost, improvements can be made. The orange-brown color of the standard fence panels so widely available are glaring and brash, but staining them with a more subdued color, such as dark green, will minimize the fence's impact, blending it into the background. Staining with a strong color and adding planed, shaped posts with finials will make the fence into a feature and emphasize the importance of the boundary.

Unattractive close-board, chain link or chestnut pale fencing can be improved by planting ivies which will grow up against it and create a green hedge. First, make sure the fence is sound, then plant the ivies at 1 ft. intervals along its length. Tie the new shoots against the fence as they are produced (see page 98) and, once the ivy has reached the top of the fence, clip it twice a year to keep it tidy and within

bounds. Suitable green-leaved ivies include *Hedera helix helix* 'Digitata-Hesse,' *H. hibernica* and *H. helix helix* 'Dragon Claw,' with its deeply curled leaves. For more unusual foliage, try either *H. helix helix* 'Glymii' with dark, gossy green leaves turning purple in cold weather, throwing up the color of the beautiful whitish veins, or *H. helix helix* 'Green Ripple' with its bright, deep green leaves, sharp and pointed, with prominent pale green veins, tinged copper in winter. Mixing several different ivies will give the effect of a tapestry hedge.

Quality softwood and hardwood fences can be tailor-made for your garden by a local carpenter; treated with a clear preservative to retain the natural

A woven willow fence makes a relatively inexpensive boundary treatment, yet it has a life expectancy of 10–15 years. Its natural appearance creates a soft backdrop for planting: the rose, the large-leaved Vitis coignetiae *and* Clematis *'Nelly Moser' are all easily fixed to the fence using plastic-coated ties or garden twine.*

For a light, airy effect, you can alternate solid wooden fence panels with open-boarded ones, though some privacy will be lost. The whole look of a garden can be changed by treating boundary fences with a colored wood stain, bringing a more innovative approach to the use of color in the garden. The blue of this fencing deepens the purple flowerheads of Allium afflatunense *'Purple Sensation' and makes the pink* Clematis montana *'Elizabeth' glow in the sunlight.*

color and texture of the wood, they create a pleasing, subtle backdrop. These specials can be designed to relate to other garden features, thereby blending the design together; for example, you could reflect the curved detailing on an arbor in your fence panels. Some European fencing products have more style and are well worth investigating; they can be seen in larger garden centers. For a lighter, more open look, although with the temporary loss of some privacy, a spaced, open horizontal-board construction is unusual. Light and air can circulate freely, which is beneficial for plant growth in a confined space, and once foliage covers the fence, privacy will be gained.

Line wire fences are often left by developers to denote the boundaries of your property and, while not being imposing, they are still unattractive. If funds are limited, or no other boundary is permitted,

I suggest creating a shrub border against such a fence, using a preponderance of evergreen shrubs such as *Elaeagnus pungens* 'Maculata,' *Viburnum tinus*, *Choisya ternata*, *Osmanthus* × *burkwoodii* and *Escallonia rubra* 'Crimson Spire.'

To mark a boundary on to the street, picket or palisade fencing is the most suitable for many small front gardens. About 3 to 4 ft. high, they are traditionally painted white, or sometimes black, but a natural wood picket fence looks most appropriate enclosing a small cottage-style garden. The open nature of a wrought-iron fence, perhaps in combination with brickwork, is also fitting for small gardens because the boundary is not too dominant; it looks most apt in a formal or urban situation. Over-ornate work, however, will tend to look fussy and incongruous in a small space.

Trellis

Trellis has much to recommend it for use in small gardens. It has a more delicate air than a solid fence or wall, providing a constant backdrop in winter and a pleasing support for vertical gardening. A long, narrow enclosed space will benefit from having trellis boundaries, as the open, airy nature of trellis will make the garden feel less oppressive. The trellis panels need to be fixed firmly to wooden posts, as with any fencing (see page 51), but growing climbers up the trellis will in due course make the garden more private. Another idea is to alternate trellis sections with panels of solid wooden fencing, to retain the open quality and give additional interest to the boundary. Panels of trellis fixed on top of a wall or fence retain seclusion yet improve the ambience of the contained garden. Fixed securely, they will last and support a wide range of climbing plants without impairing light.

Numerous standard or factory-made styles and designs of trellis are available and its extensive use can influence the overall concept of a garden. Close-set diamond mesh panels in a paved or tiled court-yard suggest a Moorish feel, while a square or rectangular design is suitable in a wide range of small gardens. Trellis is not only useful to form internal and external boundaries or divisions but also to create features within the garden, such as an arch (see page 54).

Trellis boundaries to a roof garden or balcony filter the wind and provide a degree of shelter and in many ways they are preferable to a solid barrier which, in these exposed conditions, is likely to blow down or cause turbulence. The light weight of trellis also makes it far more suitable than heavier materials for use on a roof, where the structural load may have to be limited. Using a closely woven design below waist level ensures a safe barrier with adequate protection; a central rail would give added strength and stability, and a more open design of trellis above the rail allows a better view. The central rail can be compared to the dado rail in a house, and indeed the color scheme selected for painting the trellis may reflect that of the interior furnishing. If the roof or balcony is not too exposed, a glazed window could be included in the design. You can make your own trellis structure or alternatively you could go to a specialist trellis manufacturer where you might have something made which would be quite individualistic.

Suitable climbers and wall shrubs for growing against trellis on an exposed roof terrace are given in the list on page 54. Wind chill is one of the most damaging circumstances that any evergreen has to tolerate, particularly in winter, and the plant list indicates those best able to tolerate cold winds. Local conditions will vary of course, and damage may occur even on these plants in some areas.

The square design of this metal trellis gives a degree of seclusion in this patio garden. The whole effect is lightened by the lavish flowering of Argyranthemum frutescens. A metalwork topiary frame supports the pot-grown ivy.

Trellis within the garden

Trellis panels will divide an area into smaller spaces, extending the concept of the garden room without being an overbearing, solid barrier. Unsightly views or features will be screened or a sense of intrigue and mystery created by these divisions. As a wall cladding, trellises soften unpleasant brickwork and emphasize the sense of enclosure. The uncluttered lines of precisely manufactured trellis add instant formality to a space when it is symmetrically placed and custom-made pieces can be designed and built to match the period of a property. Trellis may become an architectural feature of the overall garden design or simply be a subtle backdrop, depending how it is treated. White- or light-painted trellis will emphasize the structure and draw the eye, while trellis stained with a subdued tone will stay in the background. It is most important that the trellis, whatever its style, is in keeping with the scale and setting of the garden. A grand design with dominant panels painted white may be overpowering, dwarfing the surrounds of a small space, but a sympathetic design of formal white trellis can look most effective in a small classical garden. Trellis plant supports such as obelisks, tripods or pillars are all useful as features in a small garden but must be incorporated into the design at an early stage.

Lighter-weight trellis can be used when it is being wall mounted, since there is support from the wall and this allows a more delicate construction. Always fix trellis to the wall with spacers, to allow air to circulate behind the plants and enable interesting shadows to be cast. The light and dark effects created will enliven the composition of a bland concrete wall. Although most flowering plants require more light to thrive and give of their best, *Clematis montana*, *Hydrangea anomala petiolaris* and *Jasminum nudiflorum* should grow quite well on trellis in a shady basement area.

The use of *trompe l'oeil* trellis, consisting of a flat panel with diminishing proportions and tapering widths, tricks the eye by suggesting there is a distance that does not exist. By creating this vanishing point, the eye is led away from the skyline, altering the perspective and thus reducing the impact of surrounding buildings, which might otherwise be too imposing to screen. To create this illusion the *trompe l'oeil* backdrop must contrast in color with the panel, which should either be fitted with a mirror or have a statue or urn placed in front. Angle the mirror so that the viewer does not see his or her own reflection; it is merely designed as a painting. Equally, the dimensions of the statue or urn must be carefully coordinated with the vanishing point to make the effect work. Strong horizontal lines of brickwork behind the *trompe l'oeil* panel will detract from the illusion, whereas planting around it will accentuate and frame this focal point.

PLANTS FOR AN
EXPOSED SITUATION
Evergreens
Berberis
Cotoneaster (tall species)
Cryptomeria japonica
Elaeagnus pungens
 'Maculata'
Hedera helix helix
 'Buttercup,' 'Glacier,'
 'Goldheart' and 'Luzii'
Ilex aquifolium
Pyracantha
Viburnum tinus

Deciduous
Berberis thunbergii
Chaenomeles speciosa
Forsythia 'Lynwood'
*Hydrangea anomala
 petiolaris*
Jasminum nudiflorum
Philadelphus
*Polygonum
 baldschuanicum*
Potentilla

Making a trellis arch

Narrow passages and basements can be transformed by trellis arches or pergolas to create light, airy frames which may be stained to match the decor or painted a light color. An overhead structure, taking the form of an arch or supporting two beams, can be mounted on box-shaped uprights made of trellis which have a delicate look. The resultant light and shadow will brighten an otherwise dull area of the garden; planting becomes a bonus, if space permits and there is enough light for growth.

''Pillars'' of trellis, through which plants can climb, support beams for a pergola.

A trellis arch adds lightness to a passage; shade-loving plants would add interest.

Open plan boundaries

Enclosure gives a sense of belonging and ownership, but modern housing developments are sometimes subject to planning regulations which do not permit the construction of a physical, continuous boundary divison in the front garden and so other means of partition must be found. A small tree or large shrub planted in the corner of the garden will mark the extremity of your ground while providing an attractive focal point. *Amelanchier canadensis* or *Acer negundo* 'Flamingo' both form bushy, multi-stemmed shrubs with year-round interest; they can be pruned to retain them within manageable bounds. A small growing tree such as *Acer davidii*, *Malus* 'Evereste' or *Prunus* 'Pandora' will give a different effect—plant it a sufficient distance from the house to prevent root damage. In a very tiny space, a top-worked standard shrub, such as *Viburnum* × *carlcephalum*, *Ligustrum delavayanum* or *Elaeagnus pungens* 'Maculata,' underplanted with a group of ground-cover shrubs, will provide an architectural, year-round demarcation.

A change of surface from next door is evidence of different ownership. For example, two adjacent lawns could be separated by an almost continuous planted border of low shrubs, including bold plants for emphasis; or identical paver drives could be separated by a line of cobblestones. The cobblestone surface is not comfortable to walk on, discouraging visitors from crossing over the boundary, yet it provides an attractive variation in texture.

Hedges

Hedges are an environment-friendly form of division but they have many disadvantages for the small garden. First, they take up a disproportionate amount of growing room and, being hungry and thirsty, they often cause impoverished soil, stunting the growth of other plants in their vicinity. Privet is notoriously greedy and vigorous and should be avoided where possible in the small garden. Dealing with the clippings can also be a nuisance in a restricted space. However, you may have inherited a hedge and, though it involves more work than a fence, you would not readily uproot a ready-made

boundary. Regular feeding will ensure the continued good health of an existing hedge (see page 91), especially when it is competing with other shrubs. If the hedge has been neglected, you may need to do some remedial work (see page 97).

In rural properties, hedges are often the most common and the most suitable boundary, and species such as hawthorn (*Crataegus*), holly (*Ilex*), privet (*Ligustrum*) or beech (*Fagus*) all make solid hedges in keeping with the surrounds. They must be clipped once or twice a year to keep them compact; allow an appropriate width of 2–2½ ft. for a hedge up to 3–4 ft. tall, and 3–4 ft. width for a hedge 5–6 ft. tall. Thorny hedges such as *Berberis* × *stenophylla*, *Pyracantha* 'Red Column' or *Ilex aquifolium* make excellent burglar deterrants but in a small garden it is likely that you will need to collect the clippings, bag them and dispose of them at a local garbage dump; this is not an enviable task with prickly plants. The most appropriate subjects for urban and formal small gardens include yew *(Taxus baccata)*, box, green or variegated hollies, *Elaeagnus pungens* 'Maculata,' *Griselinia littoralis*, lawson cypress (*Chamaecyparis lawsoniana* 'Green Hedger') and *Thuja plicata* 'Smaragd.' Variegated cultivars of these will give a lighter backdrop.

Box makes an excellent subject for a clipped hedge where space is limited because of its slow growth, small leaves and tight habit of growth. Buxus sempervirens is used for a taller boundary hedge and the cultivar 'Suffruticosa' for the dwarf box hedges planted in this formal front garden. Both types of hedge require trimming two or three times a year and respond well to being fed with a high-nitrogen fertilizer once new growth starts in mid-spring.

Features for a small garden

ABOVE *When choosing garden furniture, think about the material and its durability as well as its design: all accessories should be in keeping with the garden's style. This glass-topped table and these wrought-iron chairs have a classic look and blend with the overall look of the deck garden.*

RIGHT *The placing of a statue is the key to its successful use in the garden. Here the clipped yew hedge forms an ideal backdrop for this small stone figure: tendrils of ivy are allowed to trail over and integrate it further into its setting.*

The features which highlight the softer backdrop will often be the focal point of a garden, but they may also be simply garden ornaments, embellishing the outdoor room. It would be unwise to over-adorn a small space, however, and each element of the garden—be it trellis, walls, paving, arch, seat or water—must help to keep the scale, proportion and style of the overall design. The original plan will have made provision for garden accessories such as pots, seats and statuary, and collecting these movable elements over a period of time is, for many, a continuing pleasure. Here is an ideal opportunity to give your garden the individuality which makes it unique. If you have inherited a garden or employed a designer, it may be even more important for you to add your mark. The more mobile items are easily changed, enabling you to vary the seasonal effects. Containers may be filled with bulbs and perhaps ivies for spring and once they are over, the pots of summer-flowering annuals can be brought out and the bulbs left to die away in an unseen corner of the garden, such as against a wall of the house, behind the trash cans or even under a well-clothed evergreen shrub.

Garden furniture

Storage space is often lacking in a small garden and the furniture has to be left out in all weathers, calling for long-lasting materials and sound construction. When choosing garden furniture, think about the material and its durability as well as its design, because even these accessories must be in keeping with the garden's overall style. Quality polyethylene furniture is both durable and often competitively priced, but it is not always of good design. Do not allow the attractive cushions to tempt you into buying furniture—remember that the bare chairs will spend many months on view. Hardwood timber furniture wears and weathers well and its new look mellows quickly, so a garden bench, although heavy and of generous proportions, harmonizes easily in many a small garden composition. Natural wood requires little upkeep but will benefit from annual treatment with a preservative oil; colored stains or painted wood require more regular maintenance. Wood takes a while to dry out after rain; polyethylene and wrought-iron can be quickly wiped dry.

Brightly painted wooden furnishings are fashionable in a contemporary design and even add an element of fun. The seat could match or contrast with the house paintwork and in turn mimic a painted deck or arbor. Adjacent planting then complements the whole and reinforces the composition. White always catches the eye and will brighten a dark, shady space, looking particularly effective among dark, lush green foliage and the occasional white flower spike. Black and green are more neutral and blend well into their surrounds. Dark green has a rich quality and adds a sophisticated look to the garden. The simplicity of a dark green wrought-iron table on a stone-flagged or brick patio needs no further embellishment. Informal styles lend themselves to soft colors; a blue-gray arbor, enveloped in lemon yellow roses and azure-blue ceanothus, would add charm to any small cottage garden. Remember that cushions placed on a low wall or wide step in good weather will provide additional seating in a confined space.

Using containers

The very nature of a small garden limits the available growing space, especially when it is predominantly paved. One way to extend the scope of growing and to enhance the garden with seasonal color is to use containers. The inhospitable soil full of concrete footings adjacent to a wall or building often makes it impossible to grow plants in the ground but here a large planted container, not less than 2 ft. in diameter by 1½ ft. high can introduce permanent greenery. Some shrubs are more suited to container cultivation than others (see the list, left) and, in a small space, they must contribute something in every season. Small pots and hanging baskets require more frequent watering and feeding and should be avoided if you are often away from home. In an exposed site, be sure to use a pot large enough to prevent the arrangement from becoming top-heavy and blowing over. Plants in pots are less protected than those in the ground and the roots can be fatally damaged by frost. So, before the onset of freezing, windy winter weather, protect the plant by wrapping the pot in burlap or bubble-wrap.

The pots and containers you select should preferably be in the same or complementary materials as the paving, or should tone with it. The wide range of terra-cotta and stone pots, being of a natural material, blend with most paving and walling. The hues of honey-colored terra-cotta pots used with mellow bricks, light oak-colored wood or terra-cotta tiles bring a warm tone to the garden, especially when planted with soft shades of apricot, pale lilac and delicate pink, or even a bright yellow. However, these softer colors are often evident in pots that have been fired at lower temperatures, resulting in a less frost-resistant clay, so check their durability first.

Bold stone urns look quite at home in a small garden where they may be mounted on a pedestal to frame a classical front door or act as a matching pair of focal points in a formal composition. Old stone sinks make ideal containers for alpines and, placed in a sunny corner where space is limited, they can satisfy your desire for a rock garden. Planted con-

tainers on a front doorstep always look welcoming, but they must be kept in pristine conditon throughout all seasons. Sadly, it is now wise to fasten down any containers or ornaments in the front garden or choose something too heavy to be carried away.

Sculpture and statuary

The surprise of finding a statue or an ornament partly concealed in the garden will add a distinct character to the space. As with pots, garden sculpture must blend with the overall design, whether it be a figure or a sundial, while of course reflecting your personal taste. Even a very small garden can take a bold classical statue or figure, provided the garden is formal in style. For a modern garden, a sculptor can be commissioned to make an individual piece, unique to your garden; appropriate materials include bronze, lead and terra-cotta. Empty pots, such as a large Greek urn or an oil jar, are excellent garden ornaments and require no maintenance. Large pieces of strategically placed natural stone provide a sculptural alternative and the natural colors in the rock will glisten in wet weather.

Garden structures

In a small, sheltered garden, and particularly on a roof, the heat of the summer sun can be too uncomfortable for outdoor living. The introduction of an arbor, a pergola or a gazebo will cast dappled shade and reduce both temperature and glare. A pergola or overhead beams can link indoor and outdoor rooms while providing a solid structure for plant growth. The horizontal beams should, where possible, tie in with the height of the house eaves or the top of the window frames. The view from the house, obstructed by timbers, can look awkward and unattractive, and you should bear in mind that outdoor canopies will also reduce light levels inside the house. Consider the security implications too as you may make an upstairs window more accessible. Try to position upright posts with regard to your views and choose the style to maintain continuity with the adjoining building. Scaffold poles painted black are robust yet unobtrusive and will easily support timber beams, whereas brick supports will generally be too overpowering in a small space. A combination of deciduous and evergreen planting will cover the structure all year round. For example, a fast-growing climber such as *Vitis vinifera* 'Purpurea' or *Jasminum officinale* will give instant privacy while slower species such as *Trachelospermum jasminoides* or *Clematis armandii* establish.

Metal arbors with a rounded top have delicate proportions and look effective in a small garden, perhaps encompassing a statue or a wrought-iron, cushion-clad bench. Constructed in solid, galvanized mild steel, shaped to your design and painted with a metal preservative, your arbor will be long-lasting and unique. For the less adventurous, ready-made products are available. Honeysuckles, such as *Lonicera periclymenum* 'Belgica' and *L. japonica* 'Halliana,' will soon cover the structure, their flowers emitting a heavenly scent from early to late summer. Climbing roses are also a good choice, provided you choose pest- and disease-resistant specimens (see page 100). An open-sided arbor or arch, sited over a path, slows the pace on a route through the garden. The more open a structure, the less dominant it will be within the composition.

Vertical accents

Upright-growing plants and accessories can be used to provide instant height in the design of a small garden and may be used perhaps to emphasize a turning point in a drive or to frame a formal layout. While this is a useful design tool, one or two dramatic full stops in a small garden will be quite enough. Obelisks and pillars, made in wood or lighter-weight metalwork, may be freestanding or an integral part of a large container, hosting a display of climbing plants. The heavy wooden pieces look better in a formal garden, particularly if they are placed symmetrically. Ivies are invaluable for training up pillars, arbors and pergolas, providing vertical greenery even in the shade. *Hedera helix helix* 'Buttercup' growing up a pergola with *Vitis vinifera* 'Purpurea' looks spectacular in the fall, with the bright orange leaves of the vine shining out amidst the yellow variegated ivy. During the winter, the ivy retains its leaves, enlivening a bleak garden scene.

LEFT *The delicate proportions of a ready-made wooden arbor enhance a corner of this garden, made to the author's design. The placing of the unplanted Cretan pot makes it a most effective focal point when seen from the house. The seat is placed to catch the evening sun. The open trellis roof hosts a* Clematic montana *and a scented* Jasminum officinale *which will take over later in the season.*

RIGHT *These raised beds are built in brick to match the boundary walls. It is advisable to avoid high walls in a confined space and better to have a series of smaller raised beds which create terraces of planting. The plants and their foliage, including spring-flowering tulips, euphorbias and honesty, successfully soften the edges of the raised beds.*

Topiary and top-worked or mophead shrubs, grafted onto a 4 ft. stem, will add height to a restricted planting space as well as being ideal subjects for pots. *Euonymus fortunei* 'Emerald Gaiety,' *Laurus nobilis*, hollies (*Ilex* species), *Salix integra* and *Cupressus arizonica* are all available in this form and annual clipping will keep the plant to the desired shape and size. Box (*Buxus sempervirens*) responds to more regular clipping, two to three times a year, and is ideal for topiary work. Small-scale topiary is an extremely useful adjunct to small garden design, bringing instant, green-sculpted structures to any style of garden. Pyramids and spirals will contrast with the mophead and globe shapes. Ready-made topiary is available, but a keen gardener can start with a small plant and train it to the desired shape and size over time. Trellis plant supports such as obelisks, tripods or pillars are all useful as features in a small garden but must be incorporated into the design at an early stage.

Raised beds

A change of level in the garden gives you the opportunity of creating a raised bed by constructing a retaining wall to separate the upper and lower levels, forming the front of an elevated planting space. As part of the design layout of the garden, this feature can accentuate a shape, for example a curved wall which then continues as the edge of a curved lawn or paved space; alternatively, an L-shaped raised bed may project the higher level of planting into the lower patio. Three to five courses of brickwork will give enough lift to create interest without overpowering the design, as well as providing a low wall to sit on; it will not be overbearing when viewed from ground-floor windows, which is an important consideration in a small space.

Where a steeper natural change of level is involved, the retaining wall or raised bed may need to be considerably higher, perhaps as high as 3 ft. Trailing subjects can be planted in the raised bed to hang over the wall (see the list of suitable plants, right). Evergreen planting at the lower level, in front of the wall, will further soften the structure. Within a completely flat small garden, a series of raised beds can be created simply to add interest to the design. The soil will, of course, have to be retained on all sides in this case; you cannot use a boundary fence as a retaining structure at the back of a bed, since it will not hold the weight of soil or would in any case soon rot and collapse with the dampness seeping through from the soil.

Raised beds may be constructed in brick, stone or timber. Since the walls are holding a substantial weight of soil they must be built on a sound, suitably deep footing of an appropriate thickness for their height. It is worth consulting a professional for advice on construction details if you are building a wall over 3 ft. high. The back of a brick or timber wall should be protected by a waterproof membrane so that the constant moisture does not seep through and cause staining or potential deterioration. Likewise, weepholes must be incorporated during construction to allow excess water to escape. Natural stone walls may be laid without bonding with mortar so that plants can be grown in the crevices to soften the wall's appearance.

PLANTS TO TRAIL
OVER A RAISED BED
Aubrieta
Cotoneaster horizontalis
　'Variegatus'
C. radicans 'Eichholz'
Genista lydia
Hedera helix helix
　'Fleur de Lis,' 'Eva,'
　'Parsley Crested,' 'Pin
　Oak' and 'Hamilton'
Helianthemum
Jasminum nudiflorum
Juniperus horizontalis
　'Bar Harbor'
J. sabina 'Tamariscifolia'
Lavandula
Rosa 'Nozomi'
Rosmarinus ×
　lavandulaceus (syn.
　prostratus)

PLANTS FOR PILLARS
Clematis large-flowered
　hybrids
Eccremocarpus scaber
Lathyrus odoratus
Lonicera tellmanniana
Rosa 'New Dawn'
Trachelospermum
　jasminoides

PLANTS FOR PERGOLAS
Clematis montana
　varieties and cultivars
Jasminum officinale
Lonicera japonica
　'Halliana'
Rosa 'Félicité et Perpétué'
Solanum jasminoides
　'Album'
Wisteria

Water features

Aquatic plants for a small pond
For the correct balance, include plants from each group. Quantities are given below; calculate the surface area of your water feature first.

Group 1
Submerged oxygenating plants are essential for animal life. Add 1 bunch for every 3 sq. ft. of water surface.
Elodea crispa
Myriophyllum spicatum
Ranunculus aquatilis

Group 2
Plants with floating leaves keep down the growth of algae. Aim to cover half to two-thirds of the surface.
Aponogeton distachyos
Azolla caroliniana
Small water lilies

Group 3
Marginal plants add flowers and foliage. Place in containers on a shelf 9 in. wide and 9 in. below the water, running around the pond perimeter. Use bricks as a support in a tub.
Acorus calamus
   'Variegatus'
Caltha palustris
Iris laevigata 'Dorothy'
I. pseudacorus 'Variegata'
Pontederia cordata
Sagittaria sagittifolia
Typha minima

The restful sound of running water and the life it introduces to the garden puts it high on my wish list. Aquatic plants are at their best in spring and summer, but even on a mild winter day the water can be circulating, pond life will be evident and any sun will reflect on the water, brightening the scene.

An open body of water, however small, does require regular maintenance, involving dividing aquatic plants, cleaning out fallen leaves, keeping the right balance and preventing the buildup of algae which turn the water green, as well as an annual total clean-out (see page 100); it is not for the gardener with limited time. However, there is often a spot in a small space crying out for a feature, where moving water would be most appropriate. It is unwise to consider the inclusion of a pool where there are young children in the family. A child can drown in as little as 2 in. of water.

The addition of a water feature will add significantly to the cost of creating a garden, as an electrician's bill and additional cabling have to be considered along with the cost of a pump, the liner and the aquatic plants. Many water features will require the help of a professional, especially if you wish to build a raised or sunken feature requiring structural work. However, pre-formed fiberglass pool liners can be purchased and installed by an amateur, as can butyl-rubber-lined ponds. Preparing level edges is most important so that the pond is not full at one end and part empty at the other! Pumps, fountains, filters and all the components required to install your own water garden are available at water garden centers, but a qualified electrician must be employed to make electrical connections. An armored cable electric supply should be laid to the point at which you propose to introduce a water feature at the garden construction stage.

The simplest water feature to include is a wooden barrel, approximately 2 ft. in diameter, set into the ground, filled with water and planted with, for example, *Iris laevigata* 'Variegata,' *Nymphaea pygmaea alba* and *Elodea crispa* to oxygenate the water. For additional interest, a small fountain pump can be installed just under the water surface to make a gentle bubbling sound and frogs will soon be encouraged to take up residence and eat the slugs.

The least maintenance is required by water features constructed with an underground reservoir, a pre-formed rigid polyethylene or fiberglass tub which is available from hardware stores. These have the additional advantage of being completely safe for children as there is no accessible body of water. The reservoir collects the falling water and houses a submersible pump which recycles the water back to the fountain head. The reservoir is covered with a mesh grid that is in turn covered by a permeable layer such as stones or gravel. Algicides added to the reservoir will help to prevent the water turning green and care should be taken to ensure that leaves and other debris do not fall into it. After-care involves topping up the water in hot weather (an automatic feed can be built in) and possibly draining down and cleaning the pool in the winter.

Reservoir-based features will bring the gentle sound of running water into the garden to provide a distraction from constant external noise such as traffic. A Grecian urn (see right) makes an attractive feature, as the water cascades over the rounded sides of the pot and ripples over its ridged bands. A millstone water feature is constructed in a similar way; the faint sound of water bubbling through its center is enhanced by the rings of water rippling as they move over the stone surface. Drilled boulders or rocks or just a jet of water falling onto cobblestones provide further variations on the theme.

A garden wall provides an ideal support for a mounted plaque made of bronze or terra-cotta. To collect the water for recycling you may choose to have a bowl mounted on the wall below or alternatively construct a small pool, perhaps half-moon shaped, either at ground level or slightly raised. Even a shady wall is suitable for this feature, which can be surrounded with plants such as ivy, both green and variegated, ferns, mosses, hostas, *Alchemilla erythropoda, Luzula nivea, Arum italicum* 'Picta' and *Mitella breweri*.

A water feature can be integrated into even a small garden to bring added interest and movement. The natural stone coping overhanging this formal pool edge creates shadows in the water while hiding the liner. Dappled shade helps to reduce algal growth in the pond, thereby preventing murky water; it is always easier to maintain clear water in a generously sized pool such as this. Netting the pond in the early fall will catch falling leaves and minimize the risk of toxicity due to leaves decaying in the water.

A Grecian urn water feature

Any frost-resistant pot may be used as a moving-water feature. The underground reservoir must have a greater capacity than the pot so that when the pump is switched off, water is not lost. The pump, with an integral filter, sits on the bottom of the reservoir unit, connected—by a qualified electrician—through an electric cable to a supply with a residual current device. The feed pipe from the pump is taken into the pot through a drainage hole which must be carefully sealed to prevent loss of water.

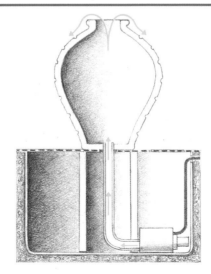

The urn sits on top of a robust plastic "collar," such as a section of underground drainage pipe of the same diameter as that of the urn. A galvanized metal grid, of approximately ½ in. square mesh, is placed each side of the feed pipe, extending beyond the sides of the reservoir itself.

The grid supports the cobblestones; a section is removed to inspect the pump or clean the filter.

Lighting the garden

I believe that we generally do not make enough of our small gardens at night. With the addition of appropriate lighting, the outdoor room can be made to work harder for its keep and give us some return during the hours of darkness. The installation of well-planned, subtle lighting enables the garden to be used on warm summer evenings and creates pleasing, year-round views from the house. The variety of interesting effects can be achieved only by the correct choice, siting and aiming of light fixtures, ensuring that glare is kept to a minimum.

Basic low-voltage and mains voltage lighting is available in simple kit form and can be installed by the amateur, provided the mains electrical connection is made by a qualified electrician. For a more original scheme, specialist companies offer a wide range of additional fixtures. Aesthetic lighting should provide a subtle ambience, with controlled beams and no stray light; the fixtures themselves should be insignificant and preferably hidden wherever possible. By using a transformer, the normal household voltage is reduced to 12 volts and low-voltage light fixtures can then be used; these are very compact and unobtrusive yet still give a powerful light source. The life of the lamp is longer and its efficiency is better, each lamp offering a wide range of beam angles which gives greater flexibility in the design. Lamp beam diameters range from 5 to 60 degrees. A narrow 5-degree beam, almost a pinpoint, projects a very confined light which is useful for picking out specific details or small features. In contrast, a 60-degree beam lights a much larger area and is useful for general-purpose lighting or lighting a large tree.

Most importantly, low-voltage electrical installation is entirely safe, even when it is in contact with water, and fixtures can easily be moved around. The low heat output reduces foliage scorch and makes the fixtures safer, especially if you have young children, as they do not get as hot. Mains voltage lighting on the other hand generally offers only spot- or floodlighting and has a limited use in a small space, though in the ground it will light a large tree.

Planning a lighting scheme

Start by selecting up to five points of interest, such as a tree, a terra-cotta pot, the steps leading up to it, some trellis and the patio. The aim is to paint a picture using dark and shadow as much as light, to accentuate the lit objects or plants. As the main feature, the terra-cotta pot may be lit with one or two narrow-beam accent lights shining from the side. To frame this focal point, light the steps by a combination of vista lighting and grazing, placing lights to cast a beam across the tread or riser. The tree may be lit by moonlighting to give a dappled effect of light, shadow and darkness. An attractive trellis, perhaps on a boundary wall or used as a garden division, can also be highlighted: a spotlight at ground level shining up the panel will create effective shadow patterns through the woodwork and the foliage of climbing plants. On the patio, aim for a low level of illumination around the table. The glow from fixtures directed at nearby plants or features will give a soft, subdued light and candles on the table would provide further soft mood lighting. The twinkling pinheads of light emitted by a specialized fixtures with a perforated shade, hanging from an overhead structure, would add sparkle to the scene.

Any form of lighting will discourage intruders and vandals, but you may also wish to add some specific security lighting. Sensor lights switch on as someone walks through the beam and are a good form of burglar alarm. To direct the beam within the confines of a small garden may be difficult, however, and there is a tendency for a passing cat to trigger illumination. The sensor could be set on a short time setting for, say, five rather than 15 minutes so that the light comes on for long enough to deter any unwanted visitors, yet switches off sufficiently soon to avoid annoyance.

Vista lighting leads the eye to a favorite feature via a particular route, be it along a path or through an arch. Low-level lights will frame or accentuate the feature and create an impression of length.

Shadowing projects the shadow of a plant or feature

As dusk falls, the uplighting in the tree and low-level illumination around the water feature highlight the focal points in this outdoor living space and lead the eye to the view beyond. Fixtures are cleverly hidden so that they do not obtrude on the effects created by the lighting. A light fixture on the house wall becomes part of the outdoor decor; it enhances the garden's living space by making it glow at night.

Accent light

Border light

Uplighter (tree-mounted)

Downlighter

onto a wall or other vertical surface; locate the light fixture in front of the plant and aim the beam up and through it. This is an interesting way of lighting a small space bordered by neighboring house walls.

Grazing brings out the texture of a particular structure or feature such as a textured pot or post, highlighting the surface graining.

Accent Spotlights are placed to emphasize special plants or features; choose the most effective beam spread and intensity. Pinpoint beams from far away are particularly successful.

Border Low-level pools of light for use on driveways, paths, lawns and within borders; this form of lighting can highlight a regularly used route so that the light cast does not detract from other garden features. Select small, unobtrusive fixtures.

Silhouetting Uplighters or well lights fixed in the ground outline a distinctive plant or feature against a lit backdrop, giving a subtle effect.

Uplighting involves lighting from below to create a dramatic effect, illuminating a structure and creat-

ing shadows. This is an effective technique when used in winter to emphasize the bare branches of trees such as *Acer palmatum* or the contorted stems of *Robinia pseudacacia* 'Tortuosa.'

Downlighting Mounting the fixtures at a high level creates general illumination for safety, security and entertaining. Can also be used to suggest a background, foreground or perspective in the garden.

Up/down lighting combines light sources from above and below to provide a glow, a useful form of lighting for patios and trees.

Underwater lighting accentuates water features or statues, but depends on the water being kept clear.

Mirror lighting uses water as the mirror by illuminating the area behind the pool and leaving the pool dark. Large trees or pool ornaments on the far side can be uplit and will be reflected on the water.

Moonlighting A gentle light is positioned high in a tree, to simulate soft, diffused moonlight filtering through the branches and producing a dappled effect below. A useful form of safety lighting.

PLANTS FOR A SMALL GARDEN

Every plant matters, especially in a small garden where space is limited, and its selection will be part of creating the finished picture. Since each plant can be visible every day of the year, they must all look good for as long as possible, if not all year round, and must complement each other. A successful planting scheme will set off the hard landscape features of the garden and enhance its overall design. Over the years, some plants will thrive, others may struggle, your tastes may change and your ideas adapt, but if the structural planting remains largely intact, the living part of your garden can evolve.

Full of color in the summer, this small garden will retain its balanced composition during the winter. Its evergreen structure is maintained by bamboo (Fargesia murieliae), Euphorbia x characias wulfenii, Asplenium scolopendrium and ivies. In winter the bare branches of the climbing rose (Rosa 'Cécile Brunner') will still tumble over the wall while winter jasmine (Jasminum nudiflorum) will give early spring color.

Planting design

The planting fleshes out the layout, or bones, of the garden, adding a particular feel and atmosphere. If the theme of the planting and the structural soft landscaping, such as trees, hedges and major architectural plants, are incorporated into the ground plan at an early stage they will become an integral part of the garden's design, enhancing its surfaces, boundaries and features. It is therefore important to prepare a detailed planting plan at the outset. I find that very small gardens can take just as long to plan as larger borders containing twice the number of plants because every plant is so crucial. But this initial plan will lay down the basic structure of the planting to which, as the plants grow, along with your knowledge and understanding, minor changes will undoubtedly be made.

The planting is often seen as the most rewarding part of creating a garden, and most people will undertake it themselves, unlike building a wall or laying a patio. It can, however, be a daunting task if you know little about plants, their habit of growth and their likes and dislikes, so it is important to find out something about each plant you are thinking of using. Selecting the plants can be compared to choosing the soft furnishings for a room, since the plants and groupings chosen will reinforce the style

created by the structural design, whether this is formal or informal, in the style of a cottage garden or one with a Mediterranean feel.

Looking at pictures can be a helpful starting point but do not just go through your favorite gardening book and list plants from this; drawings are not always accurate and photographs can be misleading. It is much better to start with some plants that you have seen and whose habit of growth, size and flower color you know, and add to this initial choice only a few unknowns.

Many of the more common plants, often frowned upon for their familiarity, can be relied on to grow well in more or less any soil or garden—which is why they are so popular. Plants such as Virginia creeper (*Parthenocissus quinquefolia*), forsythia and London pride (*Saxifraga urbium*) will give pleasure with very little effort so do not reject these, just because they are commonplace. Once you gain interest and experience, and your plant knowledge becomes greater, you can always add and experiment with more plants. Your planting plan provides the basic structure, but the best gardens are never static; they are constantly being worked on, and their planting adjusted to suit, as the living part of the garden develops and matures.

Drawing up the planting plan

Prepare the planting plan to a scale of 1:50 or 1:20 to give sufficient detail. Indicate plants by drawing circles with a cross to mark their centers; the circle's diameter will represent the approximate spread of the plant, drawn to scale. Trees and shrubs are delineated as shown, so that the smaller, herbaceous subjects that are to be planted beneath them can be indicated at the same time. You should aim to have the circles touching, so there are no gaps. Herbaceous plants can be thinned by division later.

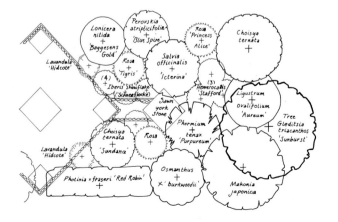

The plant spacings adopted for the initial planting plan should be based on how far each plant is expected to spread in three to five years (see page 68).

Assembling the plants

The best starting point is to consider the conditions each plant or group of plants must meet, in every part of the garden. I find it helpful to lay a piece of tracing paper over the garden layout plan (see page 29), or to write in pencil on this plan all the practical and aesthetic criteria which will dictate the choice of plants, for example dry, sunny border or area of dappled shade. I then list all the plants I like which fulfill the practical requirements of each space and which are suitable for the overall style of the garden.

Practical and climatic requirements

Even in a small plot there are likely to be variations in the microclimate and demands will vary from one part of the garden to the next. Note down any variations in the soil texture: for example, is it heavy in one part, dryer and better drained in another, is it wet in a localized depression? Indicate the aspect and the patterns of sun and shade in different parts of the plot: for example, is a wall south-facing, in which case it will be hot and dry, or is it east-facing, exposed to the cold winter wind which is likely to cause scorch on all but the most hardy plants? Is a tree canopy creating an area of dry shade, is a building overhang causing a dry, rain-free zone? Note down any screening requirements. Is there an ugly view or a building that needs to be hidden, and do you need a tall shrub or a tree? Does a large expanse of wall need to be softened and screened by an evergreen climbing plant? Indicate any special plant effects. Are poisonous or prickly plants to be avoided because of small children? Do you want the flowers or foliage near the patio to be scented?

Aesthetic criteria

Aesthetically the overall aim is to produce a balanced, coherent display through the use of plant shapes, individual flower and foliage colors, outlines, textures and seasonal effects. Note down in which season (if any) you wish the plants to provide maximum interest, in terms of flower and foliage.

For example, perhaps you would like the part of the garden nearest the front door to contain plants for winter interest, the area under a mature tree those for autumn effect and the planting close to the patio to be a mass of summer color. Or maybe the whole garden is to be foliage-only shrubs. In this case, indicate the role your plants must perform, whether they are to be climbing plants, evergreens for the back of the border or smaller evergreens for the front. What will their size be in, say, ten years? Note your preferred colors, perhaps aiming to match an interior color theme. Once you have made notes along these lines, start to consider plants that fulfill the necessary criteria. The list should not be too long as many plants will have been eliminated due to their unsuitability on practical grounds.

In this predominantly summer-flowering corner of the garden, the silvery leaves of a weeping pear (Pyrus salicifolia 'Pendula') form the backdrop, supporting clematis and a white rose. The spiky, upright shapes of lavender, iris and blue Anchusa make a good contrast with the pear. Alchemilla mollis, Vinca minor and Viola tumble over the path, softening the composition.

Separating the plants into broad categories (see page 72) will help you to start putting pen to paper. First think about the structure (trees and major accent plants which shape the garden) and the background planting in each border, so that the overall design and style is reinforced and to ensure that there will be year-round interest. At this stage of planning, minor accent plants may be worked into a plant grouping to vary the effect. Round clipped box *(Buxus sempervirens)* or *Choisya ternata*, for example, may be incorporated as the dominant plant in a group but, when surrounded by softer shapes such as *Bergenia stracheyi alba* or *Viola cornuta* 'Alba,' the effect will be that of a highlight within the group. This contrasts with the strong, eye-catching effect they could have when placed as specimens to frame an opening on to a lawn or into a second area of the garden; these plants would then become definite focal points. Around this structural planting, select intermediate and decorative plants that will enhance the design, introduce complementary plant shapes and habits, add variation in leaf color, shape and texture, and provide seasonal bursts of flower.

Spacing the plants

Twenty years may be the period of maturity for many shrubs, but planting a small garden to allow for this will leave numerous bare spaces for many years and is not practicable. Your plan should take into account the length of time each plant takes to grow over a three- to five-year period, allowing the structural shrubs room to develop in the long term yet meanwhile interplanting with perennials or smaller shrubs which will fill the spaces in the interim. For a longer-term outlook you should space structural shrubs further apart—up to 10 ft.—and plant tall perennials in between which can be removed as the shrubs grow; for the temporary infill, use plants such as *Campanula lactiflora* 'Lodden Anna,' *Phlox paniculata* cultivars and foxgloves *(Digitalis purpurea)*.

Regular pruning will become necessary for some of the more vigorous shrubs, to maintain an appropriate balance in a confined space (see page 94). It may be essential to maintain the height offered by some tall shrubs for screening, but if they are left completely unmanaged they could potentially fill half the garden in time.

HOW FAR APART?
I use a few standard plant spacings when preparing a planting plan; these act as a guideline and are based on the expectation of plants growing to cover the ground within three to five years. After this, you will need to prune the shrubs regularly.
Climbers:
    6½–9 ft.
Structural shrubs:
    3–5 ft.
Intermediate shrubs:
    2–4 ft.
Small or infill shrubs:
    20 in.–3 ft.
Infill perennials:
    1–2 ft.

An unattractive rendered wall behind this small raised bed is clothed with the evergreen climbers Garrya elliptica *and* Hedera helix helix *'Buttercup.' The white-flowering* Clematis viticella *'Alba Luxurians' highlights the summer backdrop, along with the infill plants,* Agapanthus campanulatus albidus, Anemone × hybrida *'Honorine Jobert,' hostas and violas. The balanced planting frames the wall.*

The rate of plant growth varies according to soil, situation and locality and can differ considerably within separate areas of a garden. The constricted root run under a paved area or in permanently dry soil adjacent to the house will retard growth and shrubs planted in these positions may never reach their maximum size.

Even in the confines of a small space, when planning a border always allow the maximum width possible to accommodate a row of tall shrubs at the back, medium-height plants in the middle and low plants in front. But the layout and practical requirements of your garden may well mean that you have a narrow space only suited to planting one climber or wall shrub to clothe the fence; however, there may be room for underplanting at its foot. Excessively tall, spreading shrubs—such as *Forsythia spectabilis*, *Prunus laurocerasus*, *Cotoneaster salicifolius* and *C. floccosus*—could be overbearing in a small garden, but always consider the pruning potential of the plant before dismissing it. These shrubs may also be trained against a wall or trellis (see page 98) and with regular pruning will remain a manageable size.

ABOVE *A combination of lily of the valley* (Convallaria majalis), Viola riviniana *Purpurea Group and a clump of ferns* (Onoclea sensibilis) *make a pleasing late spring-flowering composition alongside this patio. The strong shape and form of the ferns create a bold accent while the viola and lily of the valley spread and seed to fill in the spaces around the more structural planting.*

LEFT *All categories of planting come together successfully in this small garden border, highlighted by the small lead figure and birdbath.* Cotinus coggygria, *with its glistening, purple-hued foliage, gives structure while the lime-green* Alchemilla mollis *provides fullness in the center. The bright green, strap-shaped foliage of the decorative* Agapanthus campanulatus, *which will flower later in the year, highlights the delicate deep pink flowers of* Geranium palmatum. *In the foreground is* Arabis alpina 'Variegata.'

The best trees for small plots

A weeping shape of tree forms an eye-catching focal point.

An irregular, spreading shape gives shade to the informal garden.

A fastigiate shape suits narrow gardens needing height.

If you have space for a tree and wish to include one in your small garden, you should choose it at the planning stage, since this decision is a crucial one. The right tree will successfully help to shape the design, act as a main focal point and provide the desired degree of shade. An unsuitable tree may outgrow its space too quickly and dominate the garden, causing unacceptable levels of shade, or its roots may damage buildings or services, or the tree may lack sufficient seasonal interest. Unlike a small shrub, it is difficult to move a tree and valuable growing time will be lost if you need to re-evaluate and change the species.

An existing tree may provide privacy and shade in summer or somewhere to suspend a swing or a hammock, but this structural element will have more value if it also has ornamental attributes. Suitable trees can offer decorative foliage, autumn color, edible or ornamental fruits, interesting flowers and attractive textured or colored bark for winter interest. When choosing a tree for a small garden, you should always aim to select one that offers at least two of these special characteristics: perhaps *Prunus* 'Pandora' for its spring flowers and autumn foliage, *Sorbus hupehensis* for its delicate summer foliage color and autumn berries or *Amelanchier canadensis*, displaying white flowers in early spring as the copper-tinted leaves appear, and ending the year with magnificent autumn color. However, I do include some trees with only one characteristic in my repertoire since either their season is fairly long or they are particularly suitable for small spaces. *Gleditsia triacanthos* 'Sunburst' has delicate yellow foliage all summer and allows dappled light through the canopy; the striated bark of *Acer grosseri hersii* looks effective in a winter scene and although for the rest of the year the green canopy is plain, the tree is small and compact and ideal for the small garden in which foliage interest predominates.

Look in a tree book or study a mature specimen before selecting and buying your young tree to check its long-term shape and habit, which may not be evident in the small specimen offered for sale. Does your design call for a "proper tree" with a clear trunk 6 to 8 ft. tall, with a head above this, which will allow planting and walking access beneath its canopy? Or does it call for a tree that is branched and foliated to the ground? Small trees with side branches on the main stem when young can be trained into a tree with a head as they grow; others are best left as feathered trees, such as a multi-stemmed *Amelanchier lamarckii* and *Acer negundo* 'Flamingo.'

The best shape of tree

The tree is not an isolated item, however, and like any component in a small garden it must work hard within the whole space. The habit of the tree indicates the way the branching structure develops and the shape is the silhouette of the plant, seen most strongly in summer when the tree is in full foliage. Both the habit and shape of the tree must complement your chosen garden style and planting scheme and its color and shape must contrast or blend with adjacent planting to enhance the overall effect.

Trees also provide structure (see page 74) on a larger scale, perhaps balancing the proportion of a building, but they must still be considered within the overall composition. The height and evergreen foliage of conifers is useful in a small garden to screen upstairs windows in winter, since many trees will give height but few have year-round foliage. Check their ultimate height and spread before planting, as many of the taller growing conifers spread 6 to 9 ft. and will therefore take up considerable space. Some of the more upright conifers suitable for a small garden include *Thuja occidentalis* 'Smaragd,' *Juniperus communis* 'Hibernica' and *Juniperus scopulorum* 'Blue Heaven.' Remember that these strong fastigiate shapes will also act as focal points (see page 72).

A wide range of softly irregular to round-headed trees are suitable for most styles of small garden and their informal canopy does not dominate the scene. They can be enjoyed for their flower, fruit, foliage or bark and blend readily into the planting scheme, yet they offer shade, structural form and height.

TREES FOR SMALL
GARDENS
Acer davidii
A. negundo 'Flamingo'
Alnus incana 'Aurea'
Amelanchier canadensis
Crataegus pedicellata
   (easily pruned)
Gleditsia triacanthos
   'Rubylace'
Magnolia × soulangeana
Malus 'Amberina,'
   'Ormiston Roy,'
   'Red Jade'
   (pendulous form)
   and 'Royalty'
Mespilus germanica
Prunus 'Amanogawa'
   and 'Pandora'
Prunus × subhirtella
   'Fallalis'
   and 'Fukubana'
Pyrus salicifolia
   'Pendula'
Robinia hispida
R. × margaretta 'Pink
   Cascade'
   (syn. 'Casque Rouge')
R. × slavinii 'Hillieri'
Sorbus aria 'Chrysophylla'
S. aucuparia 'Dirkenii'
S. hupehensis
S. vilmorinii
Ulmus minor (*V.
   carpinifolia*) 'Dampieri
   Aurea' (syn. 'Wredei')
Wisteria
   (top-worked and
   trained as a standard)

The weeping pear (Pyrus salicifolia 'Pendula') is an excellent specimen tree for a small garden. Growing to 15 to 20 ft., with a spread of 12 ft., it can be left unpruned, to develop a very full, weeping head down to the ground, or, as here, pruned to form a smaller head which is slightly pendulous, held on a clear stem; this lets in more light and gives access beneath the tree's canopy.

Trees with an upright to fan-shaped habit, for example *Prunus subhirtella* 'Fallalis' or *Gleditsia triacanthos* 'Rubylace,' are excellent for small plots since they provide height and yet allow light beneath the canopy for underplanting. The branches of weeping or dome-shaped trees by contrast tumble to the ground and are very striking, forming a strong focal point (see page 72). The pendulous habit of *Betula pendula* 'Youngii' is softer than the weeping habit of the smaller *Salix caprea* 'Kilmarnock.'

Where the garden space is very limited in width, and height is therefore called for, columnar or fastigiate trees are extremely useful. Their narrow habit of growth is eye-catching, so use trees such as *Prunus* 'Amanagowa' and *Sorbus aucuparia* 'Fastigiata' with forethought or surround them by other planting to diminish the effect of the vertical accent. A slightly broader, square or cylinder-shaped head can be achieved by clipping trees such as *Taxus baccata* 'Fastigiata' into shape; these trees are particularly suited to the small formal garden.

The twisted branches of *Robinia pseudoacacia* 'Tortuosa' or *Corylus avellana* 'Contorta' can be extremely distinctive in winter, when they are bare, and they add a sense of humor to a composition. The contorted shape is especially effective when used in association with rocks, cobblestones and water. Even in summer the light foliage canopy of the *Robinia* allows its tortuous branches to be revealed.

Some nurserymen graft *Malus* and *Prunus* trees on to a dwarfing rootstock which will reduce their ultimate size to about two-thirds of what is normally expected. They still grow relatively quickly and, if they are fruiting trees, will produce heavy crops of fruit within four to five years. When purchasing, ask for a *Prunus* or *Malus* on a dwarfing rootstock. Remove any suckers which appear below the point of budding or grafting, because if these are allowed to grow they will have the characteristics of the rootstock, rather than those of the cultivar you have chosen.

Other trees may be small due to their extremely slow habit of growth, which does mean that you will have a long wait before the tree reaches its true "proportions," especially if you start with a small plant. Many trees can be purchased as mature specimens, but these are likely to be very expensive. Pruning trees hard from the start extends their life and gives a good, multi-headed tree—but beware of pruning too hard, or you will spoil the shape.

Categories of planting

Rosmarinus officinalis
Rosemary, the invaluable
"dew of the sea," is reputed
to strengthen the memory.
During the Plague it was
carried by people in pouches
and the hollow handles of
walking sticks to purify
them. Rosemary is a pungent
herb, renowned for its
culinary uses; its clippings
emit a lovely scent when
burned on an open fire.

I have found it helpful to group plants other than trees into one of four categories: accent planting, background and structural planting, intermediate planting and decorative planting. When preparing your planting plan, you should aim, where the space allows, to select at least some plants from each category. This will give a scheme that has: structure to provide shape, solidity and winter form; an occasional accent or focal point as a highlight; medium-sized shrubs and perennials for the middle of a group; and plants that bring interest to the front of a display or provide splashes of seasonal color.

Accent plants

Focal points will have been planned into your overall garden design and there are some plants which make particularly attractive highlights. These accent plants will provide points of emphasis, lead the eye around the garden and provide full stops or punctuation marks among the bulk of the planting. In a tiny space, there may be a need for only one very special plant and this must be in scale with the rest of the garden and the house. A large oak tree, for example, would eventually become totally out of proportion in a small space and would unbalance any

planting scheme. Sometimes an existing tree is already extremely dominant and will automatically become the focal point, so other planting must be designed around it; this may be used as an opportunity to create a miniature woodland-style planting in its shade.

In a small garden one cannot rely on fleeting, brightly colored flowers for impact—a more permanent strong shape or strong foliage color is required. Try one of the purple-leaved maples, for example *Acer palmatum* 'Atropurpureum' or 'Burgundy Lace,' or the strong form and shrimp pink spring color of *Acer pseudoplatanus* 'Brilliantissimum.' Some plant shapes naturally have a dominant effect and will always stand out from their surroundings, wherever they are planted. They will draw the eye and, if incorrectly placed, can be a visual eyesore. Picture upright-growing conifers and you will realize that this outline readily draws the eye and becomes a dominant feature. Their placing is therefore crucial and they should never be simply dotted around the garden. Columnar and fastigiate shapes are useful for framing a view and matching pairs either side of a path or garden will lead the eye toward a distant focal point. A single specimen, perhaps in a pyramid shape, is an effective way of highlighting a change of

Planting a container-grown shrub

Having prepared the soil by incorporating some well-rotted organic matter, dig a hole slightly bigger than the container; check that it is deep enough by placing the pot in the hole—the top of the compost should be level with the finished soil level. Soak the rootball of the shrub while still in the pot. Take the shrub out of its pot; if it sticks, gently squeeze the pot to loosen the soil and twist carefully. Place in the hole with its best-looking side toward the front. Check the soil level, then water in thoroughly.

Add a couple of handfuls of bonemeal to the
soil removed from the hole and mix well.

Backfill the hole with soil, then firm with
your foot to remove any air pockets.

direction, but only one plant is necessary. Fastigiate shapes appropriate for creating accents in the small garden are provided by such conifers as *Taxus baccata* 'Fastigiata,' *T. baccata* 'Fastigiata Aurea' and *Juniperus scopulorum* 'Skyrocket.'

Shrubs clipped into formal shapes, such as a dome, cone, sphere or cube, make excellent architectural features in a small formal garden. They work well planted as matching pairs, to frame a view, a feature or an entrance. Surrounded by low planting (see page 68), they will be integrated into a plant group yet still retain their dominance. Ivies grafted and trained (top-worked) to form mop-headed or weeping standards are useful accent plants either standing alone or among other plants in a border. The clear stem enables taller plants to be placed at their feet; for example, the rich lavender-blue flower spikes of *Campanula latiloba* 'Percy Piper' will add color from mid- to late summer. I find the round, dome or bell shapes of other top-worked shrubs useful for giving lift among low planting where perhaps space is too restricted to plant a large shrub or tree; they will become an integral part of the planting and not stand out as features. Top-worked *Euonymus fortunei* 'Emerald Gaiety,' *Elaeagnus pungens* 'Maculata' and *Salix integra* all add height as well as the interest of variegated foliage color to a mixed planting group.

Spiky shapes also have a strong architectural form and although there is a limited range of shrubs with this habit *(Perovskia* 'Blue Spire' is a notable one, however), many perennials have an upright, spiky habit of growth and will add minor highlights to a planting scheme. Phormiums look effective planted in isolation in gravel; they need sun and a warm location. The purple-blue flower spikes of *Liriope muscari* in autumn, the pale blue midsummer spikes of *Veronica gentianoides* or the white spikes of *Lupinus* 'The Chandelier' all add their seasonal highlight to the middle of the border.

Plants with a weeping habit can be particularly dominant and must be used with care. Grown as weeping standards, *Salix caprea* 'Kilmarnock,' *Coton-*

easter 'Hybridus Pendulus' and *Caragana arborescens* 'Walker' make very suitable features in small gardens since they are fairly compact and more shrub-like. Plants with a pendulous habit associate particularly well with water. Shrubs with a horizontal habit, such as *Viburnum plicatum* 'Mariesii,' act as effective focal points but unfortunately many of these grow too large for a small garden.

The architectural form of the pair of clipped pyramidal box draws the eye. The juxtaposition of these strong accents and the softer decorative planting makes a good composition.

73

This full display relies on keeping the background and structural plants in check. On a sunny wall, the vigorous Vitis coignetiae *will need to be regularly pruned for the* Forsythia suspensa *to grow and to flower. The green-leaved ivy will spread steadily to provide good winter backdrop. Within the border can be seen the striking foliage of* Trachycarpus fortunei, Pittosporum tobira *and the yellow* Robinia pseudo-acacia *'Frisia.'*

Background and structural planting

The planting which gives year-round structure or acts as a pleasing backdrop to the scheme is predominantly evergreen; it includes shrubs, conifers, climbers and wall shrubs. Some plants will form the structural part of the overall design, delineating an area, screening unwanted scenes, forming divisions and creating vertical interest. For example, an evergreen shrub such as *Ceanothus* or *Pyracantha* may be trained on an internal structure such as trellis to screen off a work space or to create a division, while softly reinforcing the design shape. In a rural garden a boundary hedge of *Ilex aquifolium*, being evergreen, gives year-round privacy with the prickles providing a degree of burglar deterrance. A lavender hedge

around a lawn, although low-growing, is equally structural, and brings form to the design as well as decorative value as a flowering shrub.

The structural planting in a small garden should always be ornamental as well as part of the design. A bland privet hedge can be very dull in a small space, besides taking up a lot of room, food and moisture and precluding the inclusion of other, more interesting plants. Consider plants with colored foliage, flowers and fruit for several seasons of interest. *Prunus laurocerasus*, with its glossy, dark green leaves and spikes of white flowers in spring, followed by cherry-like red fruits, provides far greater interest, besides being a pollution-tolerant species.

As well as providing structure within the layout, this category of planting provides a year-round backdrop in the garden, adding cohesion to the plant display. Left unpruned, many background shrubs have the potential of growing to enormous proportions but this should not exclude them from your repertoire since they offer useful qualities and respond well to annual pruning. Pruning from the beginning ensures a well-shaped plant that will produce healthy new growth and fit the allotted space (see page 94).

The backdrop evergreens, if carefully chosen, will provide contrast of foliage, texture, shape and color and will set off the medium-height or intermediate plants in the border (see page 76) or frame garden features such as a seat. For a non-obtrusive backdrop, select evergreen shrubs with small leaves, such as *Berberis darwinii*, *Osmanthus × burkwoodii* or *Escallonia* 'Slieve Donard'; larger foliage will tend to stand out from the rest of the planting. Fast-growing shrubs can be planted if you wish to achieve a more instant backdrop: *Ceanothus* 'Delight,' *C. impressus* and *C. × delileanus* 'Gloire de Versailles,' *Philadelphus* 'Virginal,' *P.* 'Beauclerk' and *P. coronarius* 'Aureus' as well as *Brachyglottis* (syn. *Senecio*) 'Sunshine' and *Buddleia davidii* cultivars all grow relatively quickly and will soon fill a space. They will equally soon require pruning to keep them within bounds. A compromise generally works well, even to the point of using quick growers as short-term plants in the design and removing them as more suitable species establish (see page 68).

*An old stone wall in sun is
furnished with* Actinidia
kolomikta, Euonymus
fortunei *and yew.*

Structural plants for shade

Dappled or part-shade is ideal for the evergreen *Garrya elliptica*, which provides an eye-catching display of catkins during winter. Select a cultivar called 'James Roof,' which has very long, showy catkins and which associates well with the white flowering *Clematis* 'Marie Boisselot.' *Pyracantha* is an extremely useful evergreen, covering a fence all year round with bright, glossy green leaves and providing a mass of white flowers in the summer and copious red, yellow or orange berries in the autumn and winter. If it is trained regularly and neatly against a fence, the growth does not protrude beyond 2 ft.; the sharp thorns make pruning an unpleasant task but the year-round value of the plant outweighs this disadvantage. The highlight of the year is watching all the birds feed on the berries in winter.

Boundaries in deep shade often look dismal and inhospitable but they can easily be clad with permanent background planting. Some of the most attractive evergreens are variegated ivies, such as *Hedera helix helix* 'Goldheart.' Camellias, also evergreen, are easy to train along a fence and they form a dark green backdrop with showy white, pink or red flowers in spring. The most suitable for a small garden include *Camellia × williamsii* 'Donation,' with semi-double pink flowers, and *C. × williamsii*

'J. C. Williams,' with single pink flowers. Camellias must be planted only on acid soils and never on east-facing boundaries, because the flowers will be damaged by the early-morning sun. *Chaenomeles × superba* hybrids are also excellent for full shade and can be trained on the fence (see page 98) to provide bright, cheerful flowers in early spring and a pleasant backdrop during the summer. They are deciduous and, to soften the fence during winter, intermediate planting here should include evergreens.

To add summer color to the backdrop evergreens on a shady boundary, plant clematis to twine through the green foliage and complement the display. Many clematis grow happily in some shade, protected from full sun, which can cause their flowers to fade. Some useful clematis include 'Comtesse de Bouchaud' and 'Victoria,' which flower from midsummer to early autumn, and 'Nelly Moser' and 'Lasurstern,' which flower from early summer, continuing sporadically until the autumn.

A combination of ivies and clematis (see left) make an ideal choice for a narrow passage since they do not protrude more than 12 to 18 in. beyond the fence if tied in periodically (see page 98).

Boundaries in full sun

Small south-facing gardens can become extremely hot and dry in the summer and the background planting you choose may need to tolerate extreme summer heat: *Ceanothus*, *Acacia dealbata* and *Fremontodendron californicum* are all examples of sun-loving climbers and wall shrubs. *Ceanothus*, particularly the evergreen forms, are one of my favorite backdrop plants, with their deep green, glossy year-round foliage and mass of powder-blue flowers in early summer. Clematis can be grown through it to extend the flowering season. The colorful foliage of *Actinidia kolomikta* and perpetual flowering of *Solanum jasminoides* 'Album' make them both worthwhile background climbing plants. *Jasminum officinale* is a deciduous climbing shrub, ideal for clothing a large wall or an arbor; it can become very rampant but it is essential for providing a heavenly scent through the summer. Small white flowers with a pink-tinged base appear out of the delicate, fern-like foliage. Once established, it must be pruned annually.

Intermediate planting in this border includes a pink-flowered Hydrangea involucrata, Berberis thunbergii *and clipped box.* Clematis *ramble over the shrubs to add seasonal color. Annual pruning will be needed in a small garden to keep all these plants within reasonable bounds.*

PLANTS FOR AN
INFORMAL SHADY
CORNER OF A GARDEN
Asplenium scolopendrium
Athyrium niponicum
 pictum
Blechnum penna-marina
 alpinum
Camellia 'Cornish Snow'
Dryopteris filix-mas
Hydrangea macrophylla
 'Variegata'
Luzula nivea
Viola cornuta 'Alba'

Intermediate planting

This category encompasses the medium-sized plants, largely shrubs, which will grow to approximately 3 to 4 ft. tall. They should be planted in front of the larger background specimens, grading the planting height down to the smaller plants at the front of the border. This layer, along with the decorative category, fills the space and forms the bulk of the border planting, its dense foliage also suppressing weed growth. A proportion of the intermediate planting should be evergreen; the shrubs are important for their year-round form, also providing foliage and flower color, autumn berries or winter stems. *Weigela praecox* 'Variegata,' with its creamy-white variegated foliage and honey-scented, rose-pink flowers with yellow markings, and *Philadelphus coronarius* 'Aureus' with its golden foliage, both brighten a small plant grouping, provided they are pruned regularly. In a mixed planting, perennials can be introduced as intermediate planting for splashes of seasonal color. Species of *Campanula*, *Phlox* and *Aster* all have a usefully long flowering season. Groups of perennials placed alternately with shrubs will maintain the structure.

The rounded top of domed shapes or hummocks associates well with most other plant forms and will soften the impact of a stronger shape in the border. Some of the summer-flowering shrubs, such as *Hebe*

anomala, *H.* 'Autumn Glory,' *Cistus* 'Sunset' and *C.* × *corbariensis*, exhibit these characteristics and can be used in informal planting. A range of gray-leaved intermediate shrubs will give an almost Mediterranean feel to a planting: *Rosmarinus officinalis*, *Salvia officinalis* 'Icterina,' *Convolvulus cneorum*, *Perovskia* 'Blue Spire' and *Santolina chamaecyparissus* all love the heat of a dry, sunny garden and are in scale with a small plot. Their gray foliage combines beautifully with the lavender and lemon-yellow flowers of many of these shrubs.

Decorative planting

This last category of planting consists of perennials, small shrubs, short-term plants and those that provide dramatic seasonal displays, with interesting foliage where possible. It provides the final infill and includes all forms of ground cover as well as deciduous climbers and some of the most ornamental planting of all. On the whole this decorative category requires the most maintenance.

Low ground cover

Grass is the most obvious form of ground cover, but many modest gardens do not have a lawn at all. Ground-cover plants will in fact carpet the ground in a difficult spot, such as the area below a tree, far more successfully than grass. Ivy, *Asperula odorata*, *Sarcococca humilis*, *Waldsteinia ternata* and many ferns will grow happily in the shade. Evergreen ground cover suppresses weed growth better than deciduous but, in a small garden, even ground-cover plants must be ornamental as well as functional. *Bergenia* 'Abendglut,' for example, has bold, year-round leaves which turn rich maroon and plum-red in winter, followed by vivid rose-red, semi-double flowers appearing in winter; it makes a lovely combination with *Acer palmatum* 'Atropurpureum' and *Euphorbia amygdaloides* 'Rubra' in the spring. Under a shady wall, beneath a tree canopy or in a tiny north-facing spot, the delicate leaf shape and bright green shades of ferns provides ground cover with a welcome contrast of textures from the bolder leaf shapes of *Hosta*, *Epimedium* and *Saxifraga*, as well as being a good foil for darker greens and for whites.

Decorative infill

Infill for the front of a sunny border should concentrate on plants with long-flowering interest and should always include some evergreens. Reliable suggestions are given in the plant list, left. Good leaf shape is also important. *Bergenia*, *Carex morrowii* 'Evergold,' *Dianthus*, *Eryngium variifolium* and *Iberis* all have year-round foliage and exhibit a varied range of leaf shapes.

Spring-flowering bulbs are useful for extending the flowering season in a small space and can be left to naturalize among shrubs. The best effects are achieved by selecting bulbs which complement the surrounding planting. A bold group of snowdrops, for example, will draw the eye to the adjacent red stems of a dogwood or enliven the composition of adjacent, white-variegated evergreens.

It is important to select plants which flower in the winter for shady areas since, in the absence of overhead tree foliage, there is more light available to them. At the foot of a shady wall, underneath *Hydrangea anomala petiolaris* or *Chaenomeles speciosa* 'Nivalis,' try hostas, hellebores and ferns.

Vertical infill

I always feel tempted to work a few climbing roses into a design because they have such exquisite flowers during the summer; even one or two appearing through an evergreen backdrop have great charm. The particular microclimates created in a small garden are not very conducive to the good health of roses, however; sheltered, often windless, they provide mildew, blackspot and pests with ideal breeding conditions. The roses, often competing with other plants in a tightly packed border, are likely to become etiolated and unable to fight off attacks. One answer is to avoid roses, especially if you do not wish to resort to using chemicals, but if you are a keen gardener and love the occasional rose, then try one of the perpetual-flowering New English or compact shrub roses and be vigilant about keeping pests and disease under control (see page 100). The rich pink, scented blooms of 'Pretty Jessica' or the purple and mauve blooms of 'Wise Portia' look quite at home in any mixed planting. The old china rose 'Hermosa' bears pretty little pink flowers of globular formation on a compact bush and associates well with *Lavandula angustifolia* 'Hidcote' and *Heuchera micrantha* 'Palace Purple.'

While many climbers provide structure I think of others, perhaps those adorning overhead beams or an arbor, as more ornamental. The pendulous flowers of wisteria and the almost evergreen *Rosa* 'Adélaïde d'Orléans' are displayed to wonderful effect on overhead structures. Wisteria grows exceptionally quickly and will soon cover its support; it is best grown alone since the strong twining stems can strangle other plants. It can take from three to eight years for a wisteria to flower but the scented flower racemes are well worth waiting for.

A range of climbers planted in a small garden will span the seasons with color and scent. From early to late winter the creamy white flowers of *Clematis cirrhosa balearica* set amid its ferny evergreen foliage, start off the year, followed by the almond-scented white, flushed pale pink, open flowers of the evergreen *Clematis armandii* in mid- to late spring. The blue, purple and pink-blue shades of scented wisteria flowers appear before the white, scented blossom of the evergreen *Jasminum officinale* takes over during the summer months. The Japanese honeysuckle, *Lonicera japonica* 'Halliana,' scents the late summer-/autumn air and, as the cold weather approaches, the large leaves of *Vitis vinifera* 'Purpurea' turn a brilliant crimson and scarlet.

Using color

Most people want a garden that looks colorful all year round but in a small space one has to be realistic and understand that there is room for only a limited number of plants. The best approach is to provide an attractive year-round backdrop, using evergreens which display good foliage characteristics, and to interplant these with plants chosen for seasonal interest. Aim to have a mixed border with an individual period of maximum interest, which for the rest of the year looks pleasing if not stunning. Most small gardens offer enough room to have four separate areas of planting which can provide a highlight for each season in turn. Color preferences are very personal but any color scheme should be harmonious (see the color wheel, right).

Each season tends to have its own predominant colors which can be seen in the natural landscape. These are suited to the changing light intensities at different times of year and I recommend working with them as a starting point for choosing color themes. Winter is an especially important season in a small garden viewed from the house and a background of evergreens is vital. In the soft winter light, the dark green foliage and brown branches of the backdrop can be highlighted by early-flowering snowdrops and winter aconites. Even the pale pink-tinged white flowers of *Prunus subhirtella* 'Fallalis' glow in this subdued light. Many evergreens which have gold variegated foliage tolerate light shade and will shine out in the mellow winter light. Pots containing gold and purple flowered winter pansies might complete your winter color scheme.

The warmer, stronger light of spring enhances the bright, fresh green unfurling leaves as they shine amid the bright yellow and blue flowers of spring bulbs and early-flowering shrubs. Blue and yellow makes a beautiful early-spring color combination for even the smallest space (see page 80); for example, the intense blue of *Scilla sibirica* looks stunning planted against the gold-variegated foliage of *Elaeagnus × ebbingei* 'Limelight.'

By summer the light is at its brightest and on a very sunny day pale colors tend to be washed out by the stronger light. In temperate climates, with many overcast days, a more subdued light allows pinks, blues and grays to be combined to create successful summer plant groupings. A small group based on this color scheme might comprise *Artemisia* 'Powis Castle' with *Veronica gentianoides* and *Lavatera* 'Pink Frills.' The more strongly colored hot reds, yellows and oranges combine well in a summer display but could overpower a small garden.

The warm, mellow autumn light glows through the reds, oranges and rich foliage colors displayed by many shrubs in this season. These colors can be quite difficult to harmonize with others, but the blue flowers of *Ceratostigma plumbaginoides* and the lilac-mauve flowers of Michaelmas daisies, such as *Aster novae-angliae* cultivars, combine well with them. One stunning structural shrub, for example *Amelanchier canadensis*, within a planting group may suffice to give a hint of autumn in a small space.

This eye-catching combination of hot colors includes Geranium sanguineum, Sedum spathulifolium 'Purpureum' *(in the foreground) and* Stachys macrantha *behind. The red globular heads are those of* Knautia macedonica.

A south- or west-facing boundary provides ideal conditions for this charming blue and yellow combination provided by evergreen Ceanothus *'Concha' and* Rosa *'Lawrence Johnston.'*

Colors next to each other in the spectrum, or those opposite each other, have a natural affinity.

PASTELS IN SUN
Astrantia major
  'Sunningdale Variegated'
Ceanothus 'Blue Mound'
Hebe 'Red Edge'
Heuchera micrantha
  'Palace Purple'
Ilex aquifolium
  'Argentea Marginata'
Lavandula angustifolia
  'Hidcote'
Thymus citriodorus
  'Argenteus'

HOT COLORS
Achillea 'Moonshine'
Brachyglottis 'Sunshine'
Camellia 'Apollo' (japonica)
  (needs acid soil)
Coreopsis verticillata
Hemerocallis 'Stella d'Oro'
Lonicera henryi
L. nitida 'Baggesen's Gold'
Phlox 'Starfire'
Potentilla fruticosa
  'Tangerine'
Pyracantha 'Orange Glow'
Spiraea japonica
  'Gold Mound'
Stachys byzantina
  'Silver Carpet'
Viburnum davidii

Choosing color schemes

It is unlikely that many small gardens will have sufficient space to incorporate large color-schemed beds hosting a wide range of plants, and it may be more appropriate to design a small garden with a very limited range of colors. A combination of white with a variety of different greens, ranging from the pale, bright lime-green to dark, glossy evergreen leaves and including white and green variegated foliage, will enliven any dull basement or small urban garden (see page 84). But if you love many colors of the spectrum, prepare your planting plan with extreme care. Try to group similar colors together, for example all the pinks, in one part of the garden, since this has more impact: unrelated blobs of different colors are confusing to the eye and make for a restless effect. By all means experiment, in a limited area, but generally use the well-proven formula that groups of opposite and adjacent colors in the spectrum harmonize.

The effects of different colors can be employed to strengthen the basic design plan. In temperate climates the soft light gives a bluish tinge to distant views; you could use blues and soft colors to create this effect in your garden and possibly lead the eye to a focal point or view at the far end. Hot colors provide abrupt stops and should not be used if you are trying to increase a sense of distance down the length of the garden. However, in a dark plot a bright splash of yellow, orange or red may brighten up the scene and introduce an impression of warmth. In an outdoor room predominantly used in the evenings you should avoid too many deep reds and purples, as they can seem to disappear completely into the shadows at night.

An extremely bright, sunny garden may, conversely, benefit from the use of soft colors to tone down the glare. Introducing white in this situation will cool the scene effectively, whereas too much white can in other situations make the space feel cold. Prominent groups of white-flowered plants may act as a focal point, standing out from their surroundings and drawing the eye. Off-whites and creams do not distract the eye and can be used very effectively in a colored border to make the transition from one color grouping to another.

Sun and shade

A sunny courtyard

A sheltered courtyard garden, with protection
from boundary walls, provides an ideal
microclimate for sun-loving species. This
scheme for the small front garden of a
substantial formal house would be equally
suited to a modest town garden. The hebes
and cistus benefit from the protection offered
and will thrive in hot conditions. Even more
tender species, such as *Abutilon*, *Sollya
heterophylla*, *Pittosporum tobira*, *Billardiera
longiflora* and *Drimys winteri*, will survive in
this sheltered situation in mild regions,
provided they could be given some winter
protection. The scented flowers and foliage of
myrtle, lavender and the evergreen clematis
(*Clematis armandii*) surround the entrance to
the house. The scheme is illustrated as it
would appear in mid- to late summer.

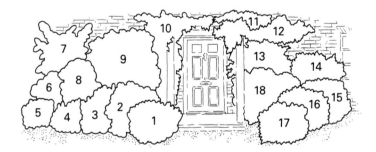

1 *Lavandula × intermedia*
  'Vera'
2 *Cistus × pulverulentus*
3 *Penstemon* 'Pennington
  Gem'
4 *Salvia patens*
5 *Diascia vigilis* 'Elliot's
  Variety'
6 *Pittosporum tobira*

7 *Sollya heterophylla*
8 *Eleutherococcus
  sieboldianus* 'Variegatus'
9 *Itea ilicifolia*
10 *Actinidia kolomikta*
11 *Clematis armandii*
12 *Clematis* 'Ville de Lyon'
13 *Weigela praecox*
  'Praecox Variegata'

14 *Romneya coulteri*
15 *Rosmarinus officinalis*
  'Sissinghurst'
16 *Hebe* 'La Séduisante'
17 *Lavandula stoechas
  pedunculata*
18 *Myrtus communis
  tarentina*

A shady basement

A sunless aspect such as this dark basement benefits from a simple, predominantly green planting and there are many green-leaved plants without variegation suited to conditions of shade. Green tends to be overlooked when thinking of color, but it is an extremely important backdrop in most small spaces. The shades of green are numerous and every season brings a variation to the color of each leaf. The most effective design can be kept muted by using low-maintenance foliage plants and little else, or it might be subtly lifted by incorporating white, as here, or cream or pale yellow. The part of the planting scheme illustrated is against the end wall of the garden; it is shown in late spring/early summer.

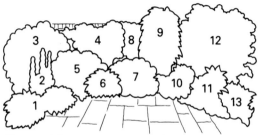

1 *Hosta undulata* var. *univittata*
2 *Digitalis purpurea* 'Alba'
3 *Cornus alba* 'Sibirica Variegata'
4 *Chaenomeles × superba* 'Jet Trail' with *Clematis alpina* 'Columbine White'
5 *Hydrangea macrophylla* 'Tovelit'
6 *Luzula sylvatica* 'Marginata'
7 *Skimmia japonica* 'Fragrans'
8 *Hedera helix helix* 'Pedata'
9 *Thamnocalamus spathaceus*
10 *Hosta* 'Ginko Craig'
11 *Vinca minor* 'Alba' with *Adiantum pedatum*
12 *Garrya elliptica* 'James Roof' (wall-trained)
13 *Convallaria majalis* 'Albistriata'

Special-interest plants

Using scent

Every small garden should include some plants with fragrant flowers or foliage because scents are accentuated in an enclosed space. Position aromatic plants so the benefit of their scents is noticed: for example, use scented climbers around a window or clove-scented pinks in a raised bed. Scented plants with winter interest should always be near the house, perhaps by the front door or on a well-used path; include *Mahonia japonica*, *Viburnum × bodnantense* 'Dawn' or *Sarcococca humilis* in your winter grouping. From spring to summer, scented shrubs can be enjoyed as you pass through the garden; place them near a seat or patio or under an open window. The compact evergreen growth of *Skimmia japonica* 'Rubella' sets off the sweetly scented panicles of flowers in spring. *Choisya ternata* produces scented white flowers from early spring, in addition to its bright green aromatic foliage. The purple flowers of *Daphne odora* 'Aureomarginata' set against its variegated evergreen foliage perfume the early spring garden deliciously. In the confined space of a balcony, where you are likely to brush past shrubs,

scented foliage is of particular value. It is worth having shrubs such as lavender, *Santolina* and *Helichrysum italicum* in close proximity. Lemon verbena (*Aloysia triphylla*, syn. *Lippia citriodora*)', *Daphne odora* and scented-leaf pelargoniums will also be appreciated but will need winter shelter.

With limited growing space, bulbs and annuals in pots are invaluable for adding summer scent. Lilies are my first choice—the highly scented *Lilium longiflorum* for sun and *Lilium regale* in partial shade. The annual *Nicotiana alata* (syn. *N. affinis*) is intensely fragrant and a small group can be grown among shrubs, perhaps taking over from spring bulbs. The taller *N. sylvestris*, which tolerates partial shade, is lightly fragrant and blooms from late summer to the first frosts. At any time from early spring to early summer, you can sow a patch of *Matthiola bicornis* (night-scented stock) near a window, in either sun or part shade, and by midsummer the fragrance of the insignificant flowers will perfume the evening air. In a sheltered small garden, where indoor winter protection can be given, the heavenly scent of × *Citrofortunella microcarpa* (calamondin orange) flowers fills the garden throughout summer and the small orange fruits adorn the evergreen foliage. These are ideal plants for pots.

There are many attractive aromatic herbs worthy of inclusion in a small space. The essential oils in their leaves and stems is released when the cell wall is broken and the scent is then emitted. The evergreen structure of a rosemary bush, the colorful foliage of gold or purple-leaved sage, the gray foliage and blue flowers of lavender and the pink globular flowers of chives all contribute to the overall design of a garden.

Plants for paving

In a small garden it is important to make full use of all surfaces for growing and this includes paved areas. Many plants will invade crevices in paving, helping to keep out unwanted weeds. *Geranium robertianum* (herb Robert) is one of the most versatile: it will grow in any crack, in sun or shade, providing a continuous display of small, deep pink, almost

SCENTED SHRUBS FOR
A SMALL GARDEN
Spring
Osmanthus × burkwoodii
  (structural)
Viburnum × burkwoodii
  (structural)

Summer
Cytisus battandieri
  (structural)
Philadelphus 'Belle Etoile'
  (intermediate)
*Trachelospermum
  jasminoides*
  (evergreen climber)
Philadelphus coronarius
  'Variegatus'
  (intermediate)

Autumn and winter
Elaeagnus × ebbingei
  (structural)
Mahonia japonica
  (structural)
Sarcococca humilis
  (intermediate)

**Year-round
  scented foliage**
Aloysia triphylla (infill)
Daphne mezereum (infill)
Daphne odora 'Aureo-
  marginata' (infill)
Laurus nobilis
  (background/accent)
Lavandula (infill)
Nepeta × faassenii (infill)
Salvia officinalis
  'Purpurascens'
  (intermediate)

magenta flowers from early summer to the first frosts. In autumn the leaves turn an attractive shade of red, complementing the pink flowers. Weeding out unwanted plants is simple, since the root system is not persistent. *Lysimachia nummularia* 'Aurea,' *Campanula garganica* and the wild pansy *Viola tricolor* will happily grow in paving on a semi-shady patio.

The harshness of a stone patio in a sunny garden can be softened by planting clumps of creeping species in the gaps. If the patio is regularly walked on, select plants that will tolerate this, such as chamomile (*Chamaemelum nobile* 'Treneague') and the carpeting thyme, *Thymus serpyllum*, which makes neat evergreen mats, covered with dainty pink, red or white flowers in summer. The silver-gray leaves of *Leucanthemum hosmariense* make a low mound, carrying hundreds of black buds which open to white daisies in spring and early summer. Where there is a little more moisture, the clumps of iris-like leaves of *Sisyrinchium idahoense* 'Album' provide a contrast in texture; *Pratia pedunculata*, *Acaena* 'Blue Haze' and dwarf *Dianthus* are just a few more of the alpines that will thrive in these conditions.

Planting in containers

In a small garden, the permanent, structural planting can be supplemented with seasonal displays in planted containers to make a real impact. These seasonal displays must always be integrated with the color and style of adjacent planting. To complement a gold and yellow winter border, add a pot full of early yellow-flowered narcissus, such as *N*. 'February Gold,' peeping through blue pansies. A low bowl full of the earliest-flowering dwarf bulbs, such as crocus or snowdrops, will provide a cheering sight at the end of winter: plant at least 50 small bulbs in a 12 in. diameter bowl to give a full display. I sometimes use a cheap fiber pot, hide it away until the buds appear and then tuck the pot among low evergreen shrubs so that only the flowers and foliage are visible and they have an instant backdrop.

A winter arrangement for a large planter or tub may contain a permanent planting of *Skimmia japonica* 'Rubella,' *Erica carnea* 'Myretoun Ruby,' and 'Pink Spangles,' *Hedera helix helix* 'Avon' or 'Perkeo' trailing over the edge with their bronze winter hues, and the gold foliage of *Euonymus fortunei* 'Emerald 'n Gold' or a trailing conifer such as *Juniperus communis* 'Depressa Aurea.' Include bulbs such as yellow *Iris danfordiae* or large-flowered Dutch hybrid crocuses.

During summer an old jug or small terra-cotta flower pot planted with *Heuchera micrantha* 'Palace Purple' adds a pleasing highlight to a garden of soft colors. With this permanent foliage you could place a larger container full of mainly flowering species such as *Argyranthemum* 'Pink Delight,' *Diascia vigilis*, *Verbena* 'Sissinghurst' and pelargoniums.

Lilies perform well when container-grown, provided they are fed regularly throughout their growing period and repotted annually. Pots of lilies can also be plunged into the ground among shrubs, giving the structural planting extended interest. Those suitable for pot culture include: *Lilium* 'Sterling Star,' white with darker spots; 'Star Gazer,' crimson; the golden yellow 'Connecticut King' and the highly scented trumpet hybrids; 'Casa Blanca,' white; 'Black Beauty,' dark red, edged with white.

Seasonal schemes

Every season has its own special appeal and even the smallest garden should include plants which will shine out throughout the year. To create maximum impact, always group plants which peak in the same season, in terms of their flowering or other interest.

Blue and yellow spring scheme

The raised bed in this corner of a small back garden is the focus of attention in spring, accentuated by container-grown displays of blue and yellow bulbs. The clear bright yellow of many spring flowers makes a blue and yellow border a natural color choice for this season. Spring bulbs can happily be grown in pots and tucked among existing plants or displayed in attractive containers. Many euphorbias display lime-green to yellow flowers in spring and make ideal additional herbaceous subjects, as do the perennial wallflowers *Erysium* 'Bredon' and *Erysium cheiri* 'Harpur Crewe.' The inclusion of gold evergreen foliage ensures year-round structure in this plant grouping, while setting off the spring flower colors. A touch of gray foliage complements the composition and the fresh green young spring foliage gives impact and contrast. The small pots of blue crocus (*Crocus chrysanthus*) and yellow narcissi are the first signs of spring.

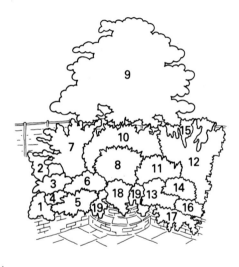

1 *Artemisia* 'Powis Castle'
2 *Rosa* 'Highfield'
3 *Hosta* 'Bressingham Blue'
4 *Narcissus* 'February Gold'
5 *Juniperus squamata* 'Blue Carpet'
6 *Euonymus fortunei* 'Emerald 'n Gold'
7 *Jasminum nudiflorum*
8 *Lonicera nitida* 'Baggesen's Gold'
9 *Gleditsia triacanthos* 'Sunburst'
10 *Elaeagnus × ebbingei* 'Limelight'

11 *Rosmarinus officinalis* 'Sissinghurst'
12 *Forsythia × intermedia* 'Spring Glory' (wall trained)
13 *Pulmonaria angustifolia* 'Munstead Blue'
14 *Euphorbia polychroma* 'Major'
15 *Clematis alpina* 'Francis Rivis'
16 *Scilla sibirica*
17 *Hedera helix helix* 'Sagittifolia Variegata'

18 Pot on base:
Scilla sibirica 'Spring Beauty'
Viola × wittrockiana
Hedera helix helix 'Eva'
Primula vulgaris
19 Small flower pots:
Crocus chrysanthus 'Gipsy Girl'
Anemone blanda
Iris danfordiae
Narcissus bulbocodium var. *mesatlanticus*
Crocus chrysanthus 'Skyline'

Autumn-color border

A corner of every small garden is worth devoting to a group of plants noted for their autumn interest. The changing, rich leaf colors of acers, *Amelanchier canadensis* or some of the smaller flowering cherries may form the centerpiece of an autumnal group. The berries on a *Sorbus* or the fruit of a *Malus* may be reflected and contrasted in adjacent planting. Observe nature's combinations, for example the rich blue flowers of *Ceratostigma plumbaginoides* set against its orange-tinted autumnal foliage. In this long, narrow garden with slightly acid soil, the centerpiece of the corner planting is the *Acer palmatum* 'Orido-nishiki,' a small, multi-stemmed tree under which other plants can be grown, some twisting up through its lower branches.

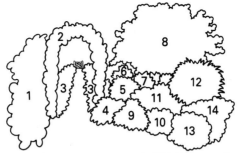

1 *Pyracantha* 'Orange Glow'
2 *Vitis vinifera* 'Purpurea'
3 *Crocosmia masonorum* 'Firebird'
4 *Juniperus × media* 'Gold Sovereign'
5 *Pleioblastus auricomus*
6 *Anthriscus sylvestris* 'Ravenswing'
7 *Dryopteris dilatata*
8 *Acer palmatum* 'Orido-nishiki'
9 *Ophiopogon planiscapus* 'Nigrescens'
10 *Tolmiea menziesii* 'Taff's Gold'
11 *Hosta fortunei* 'Aureomarginata'
12 *Miscanthus sinensis* var. *purpurascens*
13 *Euonymus fortunei* 'Canadale Gold'
14 *Aster × frikartii* 'Mönch'

LOOKING AFTER
THE GARDEN

The need to provide maximum growing and living space will place many demands on the small garden and it must be tended carefully to keep everything in pristine condition and in full working order. The garden's established framework planting must be sympathetically pruned to retain its beauty and function and yet prevent it from outgrowing its allotted space, while climbers must be trained against the wall, fence or trellis to keep them within bounds. All plants need regular feeding, and watering in dry spells, to ensure that they look their best and remain healthy enough to resist pests and diseases.

This pleasing small space in dappled shade is designed to blend into the surrounding countryside. Feeding and watering throughout the growing season will ensure the continued health of the plants growing in the lee of the large trees. Regular mowing produces an attractive green sward. The pots of marguerites (Argyranthemum frutescens), provided they are watered regularly, will flower continuously during the summer to pick up the sunlight and bring light to a dark garden.

Improving the soil

Thorough soil preparation is the key to long-term successful planting; it will ensure that the plants get off to a good start and that they continue to grow healthily. To encourage plants to produce a vigorous root system, the soil should be well drained and loose in structure. The addition of organic matter when planting and mulching after planting will increase the soil's moisture-retaining capacity. Every type of soil is improved by the addition of organic matter: heavy soils are opened up to improve drainage, light soils are made more water-retentive and all are at the same time provided with more nutrients for improved plant growth.

I am often called in to help demoralized gardeners who spend hours each week working in the garden but whose plants still seem not to thrive. The reason for this in most cases is exhausted soil which has been expected to carry on nourishing plants for year after year without receiving any feeding or improvement. Once the soil becomes lifeless, plant growth is stunted while the weeds, particularly perennial types, seem to move in and thrive. If this is your experience, a program of soil improvement, involving fertilizing, manuring and mulching, is required.

Bulky organic materials

The organic materials listed below are all excellent soil structure improvers. Their precise nutrient content is variable but they do release food slowly over the growing season and contain some trace elements (see page 91). The amounts are usually relatively small, however, and you may need to supplement with inorganic or organic fertilizers.

Cow and horse manure These excellent bulky organic materials can be obtained from local stables very cheaply (bring your own bags). The manure should be well rotted before use: storage generally needs to be for six months minimum; manure with wood shavings must be stored for at least six to twelve months. Carrying manure through the house to a small back garden is undesirable, however, and in this case it may be better to rely on homemade

compost and cleaner brand-name composts.

Brand-name organic matter This is a very convenient form of buying organic matter but is more expensive than making your own compost. It can be bought in bags, which makes life easier if you have limited access to the garden. It contains composted manure or fruit and vegetable waste and/or bark and may include some peat. It has generally been dried to some extent and is concentrated.

Spent mushroom compost This makes a good soil conditioner and supplies some plant food. The drawback is that it has a very high pH. It is vital that it is never applied to acid-loving plants and do not use it if the soil pH is already 6.5 or higher. However, it is ideal for neutral soils or those where you wish to increase the pH.

Garden compost This has the same advantages as manure and can be made, even on a small scale, within the garden (see page 90). There may not be sufficient compost to cope with the soil improvement of the whole garden but it can be supplemented with other bulky materials.

Bagged compost This is normally available at nurseries and garden centers. The composition of these bagged composts is extremely variable—it is usually high in organic matter but low in nutrients —and thus some supplementary inorganic fertilizers are recommended.

Surface mulching

Mulching around established plants is a useful way to keep the soil fertile, help suppress weed growth and retain moisture. For a low-maintenance garden it is absolutely essential. Surface mulches act as a barrier and protect plant roots from extreme heat and cold; they also prevent capping and cracking, which is particularly useful in silt and heavy clay soils. Manures, coconut shells, bark and compost can all be used as a mulch. Apply them to a depth of 2 in. and only mulch when the soil is warm and damp, not wet and cold, or dry, since the mulch acts as an insulating blanket and will keep the soil as it was at

A discreetly placed compost bin can blend into the background of a small garden, yet it will provide a source of valuable organic matter for improving the soil.

Bark can be bought in bags from retail outlets and is available in various grades. Coarse bark will take longer to decompose and my preference from the aesthetic point of view is to use a finer grade as a mulch around plants.

Coconut shells are an excellent mulching material which, once wetted, bonds together; this prevents the shells from blowing around. It is relatively expensive to buy but performs well and looks acceptable. While manure and compost will also feed the plants, bark and coconut shells contain little or no nutrients—check the manufacturer's label.

Using mulches

Most mulches last for only one year, depending on how thickly they are applied; on light soils it is always best to mulch every year. As a very rough guide, apply a bucketful of manure or compost to 5½ sq. ft., and dress shrubs and perennials every or every other year, roses and greedy herbs such as mint and chives annually—other herbs need none to little. In the years in between, you may use another medium to mulch to continue improving the soil structure. Tubs and pots will benefit from an annual ½ in. layer of fine compost or worm compost (see page 90).

the time of mulching. A disadvantage of mulches is that they can attract slugs; cats may also use them as a toilet and birds may scatter them.

Manure and compost must be completely rotted and therefore weed-free if used as a surface mulch, otherwise you will spend hours weeding during the season of application.

Digging in organic materials

Organic manures should be incorporated into the soil before planting. Dig out a "spit" of soil, fork over the next spade's depth to open up any compaction and spread manure in the base of the trench. Create the second trench by turning the next spit of soil on top of the organic matter, and repeat the operation until the whole area has been double-dug. If working in a very small space, lay a sheet of polyethylene on the adjacent ground and remove a spade's depth of soil from all over the bed, fork in manure, and replace the soil.

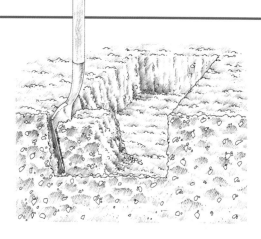

Starting at one end of a border take out just under a spade's depth of soil.

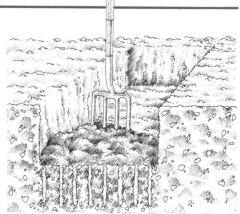

Fork a 2 in. layer of well-rotted organic matter into the base of the trench.

Jasminum officinale

These lines, written by Thomas More in Lauah Rookh, *capture the value of this climber (Arabic name* Ysmyn, *Persian name* Jasemin) *in a small space:*

*'Twas midnight—through the lattice, wreath'd
With woodbine, many a perfume breath'd
From plants that wake when others sleep,
From timid jasmine buds, that keep
Their odour to themselves all day,
But, when the sunlight dies away,
Let the delicious secret out
To every breeze that roams about.*

Compost making

Since rotted organic matter is so essential for successful gardening, enhancing the soil's fertility and structure, you should consider making space for a compost heap to recycle garden and kitchen waste, however small your garden. It is preferable to have access all around the bin but this will be governed by the available space. You can make a wooden, wire-mesh or buy a polyethylene compost bin to keep the heap together and tuck it away in a corner of the garden. Ideally the size should be about 4 ft. square but in my small garden I have a polyethylene circular bin, 2 ft. in diameter, which takes all the annual weeds, spent bedding plants, non-woody prunings, kitchen waste and even the soiled sawdust from the rabbit hutch. A removable slatted front to the bin makes emptying an easier task.

Woody material takes a long time to break down and is best avoided unless you have used a shredding machine to cut it up into small pieces. Diseased material and mature perennial weed roots should not be composted since they take a long time to decompose and there is a risk of spreading them around the garden. Also avoid evergreen material and use autumn leaves on the compost only in small quantities, collecting the remainder and storing it separately for leaf mold if space permits. Annual weeds and the leafy part of many perennial weeds make good compost. Any seed heads and persistent roots can be cut off and disposed of. Grass clippings can be added to the compost heap but must not exceed a quarter of the contents; they should be well mixed into the heap, otherwise they become compacted and the lack of air will cause the heap to go smelly and slimy and good compost will not be made. Food other than fruit and vegetable peelings should also be avoided as this can encourage rats.

To start the compost heap, put some dry, twiggy material over the base to allow air to enter the bin. On top of this place a 10 in. layer of composting material, then a sprinkling of activator; this could be a bought bacterial or herbal product or well-rotted manure or compost. Repeat these layers until the bin is full. Finally, cover it to retain heat and prevent the compost from getting too wet.

The composting process is carried out by myriad tiny organisms working on the decomposition of the organic matter you place in the bin. They need air, warmth and moisture to work effectively. In cold weather the process will be slower than in warm weather. Siting the bin in a warmer part of the garden will increase activity, thus compost will be made more quickly—but it should not be placed in full, hot sun. Turning the compost heap regularly also speeds the rotting by incorporating more air, but this is not essential. The whole process takes anything from two months up to a year or more, depending on the ingredients and the treatment. The compost is ready when it becomes dark and crumbly and the original ingredients are no longer recognizable. It is usable for burying (not for mulching) if still stringy and lumpy but an ideal compost will have broken down to a fine, crumbly texture.

Worm compost

From my experience a wormery is not essential if you have a compost heap, and you may not have enough room for both, but it does produce a little extra-fine compost and liquid food and the worm compost is excellent for potting and container growing.

A wormery is simply a polyethylene bin which allows liquid to drain from the base. A layer of bedding, that is mature compost, is covered with a 4 in. layer of kitchen waste and tender garden trash, such as thinnings and soft growth; a piece of damp newspaper is then placed on top of this. When each layer has been eaten by the worms introduced to it, more waste can be added; the worms are placed on top but work their way through the layers, after which they stay on the bottom. Avoid too much citrus peel and be sure not to use meat since this will encourage flies.

As with compost-heap microorganisms, the worms are less active in cold weather, so it is important not to overfeed them during the winter months. Typically the wormery takes 12–24 weeks to fill, after which you can empty out the fine compost and start the process again. Save the worms to reintroduce them. The liquid feed can be drained off regularly by means of a tap; it makes a nutritious plant food when diluted with water.

Feeding and watering

Reel-mounted hoses help to keep the small garden looking tidy. A decorative watering can may be left outdoors when not in use.

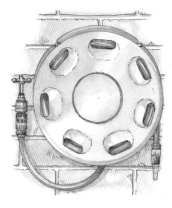

Wall-mounted hoses

Floor-standing hose reel

Ornamental watering can

During the growing season a regular supply of nutrients must be available in the soil for healthy plant growth and even a well-manured soil may need some supplementary feeding at the peak of the growing season. While bulky soil improvers are indispensable, however small the space, they may be impractical for continued plant feeding and inorganic, or artificial, fertilizers may be used instead. The main nutrients in plant food are nitrogen (N), phosphorus (P) and potassium (K); they are often listed on a packet as a ratio and always in this order. For example, a general-purpose fertilizer may have an analysis of 20:20:20. A feed to boost spring growth will have a high-nitrogen content, such as 25:15:15, whereas an autumn feed will contain less nitrogen, for example 12.5:25:25.

Plants also require minor nutrients such as magnesium, iron and copper. Trace-element fertilizers are mainly used as a single top-off to counteract a deficiency, such as leaf discoloration or some growth defect. They are applied as a foliar feed—that is, mixed with water and sprayed or watered on to the leaves. Mineral absorption is also affected by the level of acidity or alkalinity of the soil. For example, iron deficiency quickly occurs in acid-loving plants growing on an alkaline soil and manifests itself by inter-veinal chlorosis, or yellowing, and general sickness. Sequestered iron will add the missing trace element but, as a long-term remedy, the soil must be made acid for these plants to flourish; ideally, you would not grow acid-loving plants here.

Slow-release fertilizers containing nitrogen, potassium, phosphorus and minor nutrients are ideal for a small garden and will feed the plants for up to a year. They are applied as a top dressing which simply involves spreading the granules over the surface of the soil at the rate recommended by the manufacturer. Permanently planted pots can be top-dressed in the spring: remove a layer from the top of the existing compost (as much as possible without damaging roots), add a slow-release fertilizer in granules, then refill to just below the top with fresh compost. If you intend to use an ornamental mulch,

this should be applied after fertilizing. Instant-release fertilizers must be applied throughout the growing season, as directed on the packet. A non-bulky organic fertilizer such as bonemeal is valuable for spreading around new plants, to help them get started.

Watering your plants

Without water plants cannot grow. However, some species will be more tolerant of dry shady or dry sunny conditions than others and it is always advisable to select your plants accordingly. Note their performance in winter conditions—in a small garden, very dry and sunny soil in summer can become sunless, damp soil in winter. The most critical times for watering are during the establishment of newly planted gardens and during the main growth periods. Spring and early summer are the main growth periods for most plants and adequate watering will encourage new growth and the production of flower buds. Watering with hoses and sprinklers in a haphazard way is wasteful, since much of the water does not reach the roots of the plant. A good periodical soak is far better than several short bursts of watering: apply the water directly to the root zone rather than sprinkling it lightly over the foliage. Unless water penetrates the soil to a good depth, shallow rooting is encouraged, leading to a subsequent dependency on frequent watering. If you have a long period without rain, you will need to go around with a watering can or a hose, watering those plants most in need, and especially those in containers. Evergreens will generally suffer more than deciduous shrubs in drought periods; therefore watering these should be a priority.

Plants in containers will undoubtedly require occasional watering in the winter, but not during frost. The canopy of foliage can prevent rain penetrating to the plant's rootball, yet transpiration through the leaves continues. Good drainage is essential in containers as a waterlogged rootball may expand in frosty weather and crack the pot.

Lawn care

RESEEDING

BARE PATCHES

● Cut the remains of the damaged sod out of the worn area and loosen the soil beneath it.

● Fill the hollow with fine soil or soil-based compost until it is level.

● Sow grass seed at a rate based on 1½–2 oz. per sq. yard.

● Sift loam-based fine compost over the seed and protect it from the birds with stretched lines of cotton thread.

A lawn in a small garden will receive far more wear per square yard than its counterpart in a large space. Provided you have selected the correct grass mix initially (see page 47), regular maintenance will improve the lawn's ability to withstand this degree of regular use. Varying amounts of shade from trees or garden structures will affect the growth of the grass, however, and a damp sward, with less vigorous growth, allows and encourages moss to establish. Lawns in dense shade may be completely taken over by moss, at which point it is advisable to use an alternative ground cover (see page 76) or pave over the area instead (see page 42).

Cutting heights

The shorter the lawn is kept in summer, the more quickly it will become brown in periods of drought and the less resistant it is to hard wear. In winter a short lawn is more likely to be subject to frost damage. For a fine lawn with a bowling-green finish, cut to a height of about ½ in. every week during the growing season. For a lawn which receives lots of use from children, or sport, cut to a height of 1 in. each week.

At the end of the growing season, allow the lawn to remain about 1 in. long for the duration of the winter. The following spring, after applying a high-nitrogen spring feed which encourages the lawn to put on a lot of soft new growth, do not cut too short. Because this growth is soft and susceptible to late frost damage, leave the lawn at a length of 1 in. until the weather gets warmer.

Lawn management

To remove surface debris, rake the lawn over vigorously (scarify it) in two directions. This will also help to improve drainage and sod growth. If moss is prevalent, it is advisable to try and kill off most of this, using a brand-name remedy, before scarifying, to prevent spreading it further. After scarifying and dealing with the moss in autumn or spring, apply the appropriate lawn fertilizer, following the manufacturer's instructions about how much to use per square yard. Autumn feeding will only be required if the sod has suffered severely from drought or compaction during the summer months, and is therefore looking sparse and thin by the end of the summer season.

The carpet of green provided by an open stretch of lawn, albeit small, gives softness to this back garden designed by the author. Its flowing shape is an important element in the garden's layout and at the same time means a practical approach to maintenance, by avoiding awkward corners. The edges need to be clipped weekly; in addition, not allowing plants to overhang the lawn will prevent dead patches of grass.

DEALING WITH DISEASES IN LAWNS

Fairy rings: a fungus evident in late summer and autumn, seen as a curved band of lush green grass, sometimes with a ring of tiny toadstools. Control with a fungicide.

Red thread: in late summer or autumn, areas of grass turn a pinkish color, causing unsightly bleached patches. Scarify to remove dead material, then feed with sulfate of ammonia in spring and summer to increase the level of nitrogen in the soil. If they persist, apply a fungicide.

Dollar spot: golden brown or straw-colored patches appearing in humid weather in late summer. Feed with sulfate of ammonia in spring and summer; if it persists, apply a fungicide.

Dog damage: small brown-colored dead patches surrounded by a ring of dark green. Water the patch copiously after contamination.

The high canopy of the apple tree allows maximum light to the lawn below it: this will help to alleviate potential problems with damp and moss and facilitates mowing. This lawn is cut with a mower which incorporates a roller, to produce the striped effect.

All sod, especially in shady or damp areas, will benefit from autumn aeration—that is, making holes in the soil to allow air through to the roots and to improve drainage. Use a fork or small machine with spikes or hollow tines for this task; also available are spiked foot-shaped plates to attach to your boots—a human-operated lawn spiker. Then brush in sharp sand or compost to help retain the open texture you have created. If you need to reseed any bare areas, do this in spring (see far left).

Weed and disease control

A healthy, well-tended lawn will be less susceptible to disease and with a vigorous, tight-knit sward there will be less room for weed invasion. Provided you start a new lawn on perennial-weed-free ground, and lay the slightly more expensive, good-quality cultivated sod, the weed problems should be minimal. Indeed, you may not be averse to a few lawn "weeds" or wild flowers; I certainly enjoy a sporadic display of daisies in spring. But if your aim is to have a perfect show lawn, then weed control will be essential. Herbicides are present in some spring and autumn feeds, but you may also need to apply selective lawn herbicides. The most troublesome perennials are those that adapt to survival with close

mowing, for example clover, daisies, speedwell and plantain. If you want a perfect lawn, apply a specific herbicide or a fertilizer containing an herbicide in the spring, following the manufacturer's instructions. Small infestations may be treated with spot applications. Annual weeds in a newly sown lawn will be eradicated by regular mowing. Rosette-forming weeds can be removed by hand in a small space if you prefer to avoid chemicals. Remember never to put lawn mowings to which you have applied herbicide on the compost heap, or you will have problems if it is later used on the garden.

Discolored, brown or yellow patches often indicate the presence of disease. You should consult a lawn care book or take a sample to your local garden center for identification if you are uncertain, and then treat with the appropriate fungicide. Make sure that any browning is not simply due to drought, however. During dry spells in the summer, even if you have adjusted the height of cut to a longer length, the lawn may still go brown due to drought. Grass is amazingly tolerant and will generally recover with a good shower of rain or watering. If water is restricted, the lawn should be the lowest priority, since it will usually recover, whereas drought-affected plants in the border may not.

Pruning shrubs and climbers

In a small garden there is no room for plants that do not contribute fully to the overall effect of the design. It is therefore essential to understand the best way to keep plants to a manageable size that is appropriate for the space and to encourage the renewal growth which will prevent shrubs from becoming unattractive and woody. An untended leyland cypress hedge (× *Cupressocyparis leylandii*), for example, will spread in height and width and cannot then be cut back without losing the green foliage, as it does not resprout from old wood; if it is trimmed annually, however, the height and spread will be kept to the size required and the hedge will look green, neat and tidy. Similarly, to screen and to camouflage boundaries, we often select vigorous growing, large shrubs such as *Photinia* or *Cotoneaster* which, if left untended, may ultimately grow to 16 ft. or more in height and spread. While in a large garden this is fine, in a small space these shrubs must be selectively cut back to keep them within bounds.

Some plants respond more effectively to regular shaping than others but generally, with care and discretion, most plants can be lightly pruned or shaped. Among the few plants I would avoid pruning are *Daphne odora* 'Aureo-marginata,' *D. mezereum*, *Cordyline australis*, *Genista pilosa*, *Magnolia stellata*, *Pleioblastus auricomus*, *Hibiscus* species, *Thuja occidentalis* 'Sunkist,' *Phormium* species, *Sarcococca* species and dwarf evergreen azaleas.

There are other good reasons for pruning. Pruning newly planted shrubs will encourage bushy growth, with multiple branching from the base, and a shapely plant in the long term. Maintaining a well-shaped but open shrub will also allow more air circulation and prevent individual plants competing for light and space. Too much competition causes growth to become etiolated, pale and leggy, weakening the plant. A weakened plant is obviously more susceptible to disease. Cutting foliage or flowers for indoor arrangements is often a good way of keeping a shrub within bounds without wasting any attractive greenery.

When and how to prune

Always use a sharp pair of shears to prune shrubs and make a clean cut each time (see page 97). The best time of year to prune is when this allows the plant the maximum growing period before flowering. Start by noting the flowering time of the shrub and build up your plant care records (see below) as a reminder. There are a few general guidelines:

Plant care notes

I prepare a set of plant care notes for each of my clients to help them establish a regular plant maintenance routine, rather than leaving plants unattended until the garden looks a mess and remedial pruning and care become essential. Studying plant labels in the garden center and reading gardening books and magazines will help you to build up your own set of notes. As a memory jogger, summarize by season all the plants which require some attention at a particular time of year. The notes may read as shown, right.

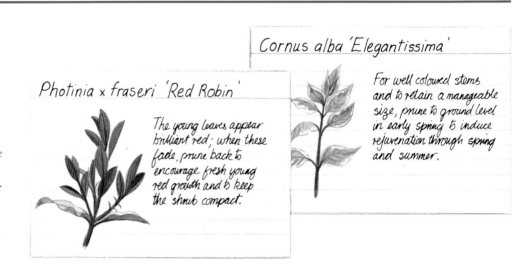

Photinia x fraseri 'Red Robin'

The young leaves appear brilliant red; when these fade, prune back to encourage fresh young red growth and to keep the shrub compact.

Cornus alba 'Elegantissima'

For well coloured stems and to retain a manageable size, prune to ground level in early spring to induce rejuvenation through spring and summer.

Regular pruning is essential to maintain the balanced composition of this planting. Lavender requires pruning in mid-spring and again when the flower spikes fade. The box should be clipped with shears two or three times a year, while one thorough pruning and a tidy in late spring will maintain the compact habit of the backdrop ivy. Training climbing roses on vertical supports such as these pyramid frames gives them more growing space and adds height to the overall design.

Deciduous shrubs which flower in spring and early summer, such as *Philadelphus*, *Forsythia* and *Weigela*, flowering on the current year's wood, should be cut back as soon as possible after the flowers have faded. Completely remove the flowering shoots back to the old wood, take off any dead or weak growth and shape the shrub to retain its balanced appearance.

Deciduous shrubs which flower in summer and early autumn, such as *Fuchsia*, *Buddleia davidii* cultivars, *Ceanothus* 'Gloire de Versailles' and *Caryopteris* × *clandonensis* 'Kew Blue,' flowering on one- or two-year-old or older wood, should be pruned in early spring, when you see the buds begin to swell. Cut the flowering shoots back hard to within one or two buds of where they join the old growth. Remove any dead or weak growth and shape as required.

Flowering evergreen shrubs can be pruned at the same times as deciduous shrubs, depending on when they flower, but generally they should be treated less drastically. For example, *Hebe* 'Red Edge,' *H. rak-* *aiensis* and *H.* 'Autumn Glory' should be trimmed lightly in early spring to induce new growth. Mature *Cistus* should be trimmed back in spring, removing one-third of the oldest growth to ground level. *Escallonia* should have one-third of the old flowering wood removed in late summer, after the main flowering period. Three to four-year-old specimens of *Ceanothus impressus* and *C.* 'Delight' should be pruned by cutting the shoots back by one-third after they have finished flowering.

Evergreens grown for their foliage such as *Elaeagnus pungens* 'Maculata' and cultivars of *Hedera helix helix*, *Prunus laurocerasus* and *Ilex aquifolium*, as well as conifers, should be pruned in early spring, before new growth begins, or even the end of spring in colder areas, and with less hardy evergreens, before growth becomes vigorous. In general, prune lightly to maintain the shape. Never cut beyond the green growth of conifers (except yew) as they tend not to regenerate. Remove shoots that have reverted to green on variegated shrubs as soon as you see them.

How much to take off

The amount of wood you remove will vary according to the age and size of the plant. Practical experience, and achieving successful results, is the best way to gain confidence. At first, if in any doubt, remove just a small amount of wood overall and, if you need to, prune a little harder next year. Do remember that where you cut, the growth will generally be more vigorous. Therefore, if a plant is weak on one side, it may help to prune the weak side drastically to encourage it to grow more vigorously.

Some shrubs will respond particularly well to very hard cutting back, where they are reduced almost to ground level; they will then regrow from the base. Yew (*Taxus* species), cherry laurel (*Prunus laurocerasus*) and dogwoods (*Cornus* species and cultivars) can be cut right back to the woody trunk and will happily regrow, producing fresh young new shoots. This drastic pruning can be very useful in a small space and enables potentially large plants with attractive foliage to be included in the planting scheme. The silver leaves of *Salix rosmarinifolia* and the pink and white variegated foliage of *Acer negundo* 'Flamingo' provide an attractive backdrop to summer flowers; both can be cut hard back annually in spring and trimmed in midsummer.

Newly planted shrubs seldom require pruning, except for the removal of crossing branches or damaged shoot tips. In spring, when new growth has begun, cut back any frost-damaged or dead shoots to a healthy bud. If a newly planted shrub is an unbalanced shape, however, cut back the long shoot in proportion to the other shoots, to encourage bushy growth from the base.

With an untidy shrub that is clearly overgrown, observe the recommended pruning times, then lightly reduce the size of the bush all over. Many mature shrubs will benefit from the removal of one-third of the growth (down to ground level) each year, to ensure a continuing supply of young healthy growth from the base of the plant. Old, untended shrubs become very bare at the base and if you inherit an overgrown garden the shrubs may well need very hard pruning of many of their branches down to ground level to bring them back into shape. But some shrubs, like lavender and ceanothus, will not regrow from old wood. Check in a detailed pruning manual before taking drastic action.

Pruning clematis

Clematis are extremely useful plants for a small garden, as they take up very little space and can be grown through shrubs, extending the flowering season. By observing the flowering time of the plant and the size of its flowers, you should be able to decide which of the methods below to adopt.

No pruning The early to midsummer flowering hybrids, such as 'Hagley Hybrid,' 'Pink Champagne,' 'The President' and 'Elsa Spath,' which generally have large flowers, do not need pruning. As a rule of thumb these are clematis which have commenced flowering before midsummer. Simply tidy and thin the end shoots back to the main framework if you wish, after flowering.

Pruning hard The late-flowering hybrids such as 'Perle d'Azur' and 'Victoria,' which also generally have large flowers, commence flowering later in the year, after midsummer. Prune by cutting down hard to 6–12 in. from the ground in early spring, cutting just above a pair of strong leaf axil buds. If the clematis is grown through a tree or shrub, provided five or six substantial stems are intertwined with the branches of the host you can prune to the branch level, to eliminate training the clematis back into the tree next growing season. Prune the late-flowering clematis species with small flowers, such as *C. orientalis*, in the same way.

Optional pruning With hybrids that flower both early and late, such as 'Beauty of Worcester', 'Henryi' and 'Carnaby,' generally producing large flowers in early summer and early autumn, pruning is optional. If you wish to prune to keep the clematis tidy, do so in mid-winter as described for late-flowering hybrids. The large early-summer flowers may be lost for one year but the plant will give a good show of smaller flowers later on. You may also reduce the overall growth by one-third in spring. The small-flowered species blooming in early summer, such as *C. montana*, should be trimmed back almost to the base of the shoots which have borne the flowers, immediately after flowering.

WHEN TO PRUNE

Spring
Buddleia davidii
Ceanothus (deciduous)
Chaenomeles
Choisya
Cistus
Cornus
Cotinus
Cotoneaster
Cytisus
Elaeagnus
Euonymus
Forsythia
Garrya
Hebe
Hedera
Hydrangea
Ilex
Jasminum
Laurus
Lavandula
Lonicera
Mahonia
Pachysandra
Perovskia
Phlomis
Pittosporum
Potentilla
Ribes
Solanum jasminoides
Vitis

Mid- or late summer
Philadelphus
Pyracantha
Weigela
Wisteria (and mid-winter)

Autumn
Escallonia
Magnolia
Pyracantha
Most conifers

Species flowering in late summer and autumn
These mainly small-flowered clematis, including the viticella types such as 'Minuet' and 'Etoile Violette,' should be pruned back as the buds begin to swell in late winter/early spring, cutting back severely, almost into the old wood. This also applies to *C. florida bicolor* and *C. texensis* 'Gravetye Beauty.' Leave unpruned, however, if there is sufficient room.

Pruning climbing roses
No pruning is required for the first two years after planting. In subsequent years, in late winter, cut back the short side shoots that produced last year's flowers and remove some of the older main growth as well as anything that is weak or dead. The aim is to leave an elegant climber with sufficient, but not excess, growth, without allowing it to become too old and twiggy. Training the strong main shoots out horizontally will encourage the production of more lateral shoots, and thereby increase the flowering potential of the rose.

Pruning wisteria
As your plant grows, train the main stems out (see page 98) against the wall to establish the framework. Prune all tendrils in late summer to within 9–10 in. of the main stems which form the framework. In mid- to late winter, shorten side shoots to within one or two buds from the point of origin.

Pruning a wall-trained shrub
The timing of pruning will be based on the general rules for the particular plant (see the list of suitable shrubs on page 98). In addition, the removal of any forward-protruding growth and any crossing branches will help to maintain the desired shape.

Hedge pruning
In a small garden it is most important to cut back or clip a hedge regularly from the time of its planting onward. This will keep it well leaved, particularly at the base, yet compact, so that it forms a solid barrier of minimum width. Clipping the sides of a young hedge will help to keep it narrow yet full; the leader, or topmost growing shoot, of each plant should be encouraged to grow straight upward until the desired height is reached. In pruning an established hedge of the required height, aim to cut to a tapered shape, making the hedge slightly wider at the base than at the top so that it is less susceptible to wind and snow damage. Cut with an electric hedge trimmer or shears once or twice a year.

Low, internal hedges should be pruned at least twice a year—*Lavandula* species in spring and immediately after flowering, and *Santolina chamaecyparissus* in spring and once or twice during the summer. Trim *Buxus sempervirens* 'Suffruticosa' and *Lonicera nitida* two or three times through the growing season.

REMEDIAL HEDGE TREATMENT
- Neglected or overgrown established hedges may need severe pruning to restore their original shape. This is best done in spring, just before plants make new growth.
- Follow by heavy mulching with rotted organic matter and watering during dry spells in summer.
- Coniferous hedges, with the exception of yew (*Taxus baccata*), will not regrow if cut back hard.
- If the ground is waterlogged, loosen the compacted earth and incorporate gravel or coarse sand to make the soil a more open texture.
- If disease is present, do not replant with the same species of hedge.

Pruning a spring-flowering shrub

To prune a healthy, mature spring-flowering shrub, such as forsythia, remove up to one-third of the wood which carried flowers in the previous season, once the shrub has finished flowering. This thins the plant and will encourage the continued production of new growth and vigorously flowering wood from lower down the plant. To rejuvenate an overgrown, neglected shrub, remove one-third of the old growth in the spring of year 1 and repeat in the spring of years 2 and 3, when the last of the old growth is removed.

Always cut back to a side shoot to promote vigorous new growth.

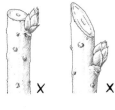

PRUNING CUT
Using sharp shears, make a clean cut just above a bud, and sloping away from it at the correct gentle angle, as illustrated here. More sharply angled cuts, horizontal cuts or cuts sloping toward the bud will cause damage by directing excess moisture toward the point of growth.

Training climbers and wall shrubs

There are several methods of training climbers to walls, fences and trellis to keep them within bounds and prevent them from becoming straggly. Wall shrubs trained in the shape of a fan (see below) may be supported in a similar fashion. Use plastic-covered wire twist-ties or soft string to attach the plant to its support; alternatively, you could use strips cut from nylon tights. These make strong ties that do not rot and will not chafe the plant stems.

Using vine eyes and wires

Screw in vine eyes at 18 in. intervals up the wall or fence from ground level to the height required. Place them 6 ft. apart. Wires may be added as the plant grows, rather than installing them all at the start; on the other hand, you may find it easier to install them against a bare fence or wall than to reach through other plants once the climbers are becoming established. Stretch a strong wire, either galvanized or plastic-coated, between each line of vine eyes. On a long expanse of wall or fence, a system of tension bolts may be necessary to create a secure climbing frame. If you need to do any painting or maintenance work, the wire can easily be cut and detached, and the plant laid down away from the wall or fence without causing any damage.

Using plastic netting

Plastic netting, with a minimum mesh of 1 in. width, can be secured to the face of a wall or fence, either by vine eyes or by screwing 2 in. thick wooden battens to the boundary and attaching the netting to them with hooks. The fixing itself must be secure, since it takes the full weight of the plant. Vine eyes and battens both allow air to circulate between the plant and the wall or fence, helping to minimize attacks of fungus disease such as mildew. Extra netting can be added as required. When the wall requires painting, detach the netting and lay this down, with the plant attached.

Using wooden trellis

Trellis is attached to a wall by means of 2 in. thick wooden battens to support the weight of the plant. The life expectancy of treated wooden trellis is approximately 10–15 years. Unless the trellis forms part of the garden design, opt for an unobtrusive, simple style with a square or diamond mesh.

Vertical wires

On a pergola, install vertical wires from the top to the bottom of a post, using vine eyes at intervals not exceeding 6 ft.

Wall-training a shrub

A wide range of shrubs can be trained against a wall, fence or trellis so that the branches radiate from the base, forming a fan shape. This reduces the amount they project forward, giving more space for growing other plants in the confines of a small garden. You must start off with a multi-stemmed plant so the training process starts immediately; at regular intervals during the growing season, tie the new growth into the support to maintain the shape and remove any forward-growing branches.

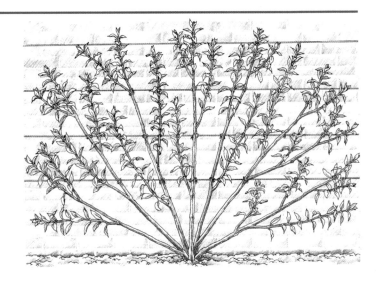

Garden hygiene

Clematis jackmanii *and*
Vitis vinifera *grow against*
a stone wall on an
attractive trellis support.

A regime of regular feeding, pruning and dead-heading will give plants the best chance of staying healthy and not succumbing to pests and diseases. Plants growing in the correct situation where they are not under undue stress will be the most robust. Always start off with healthy, young, vigorous stock from the nursery and keep all plants watered in dry spells, but do not over-water them.

Weed control

If you are starting a garden from scratch you will have to eradicate any perennial weeds before creating borders or a lawn. It is important to kill off all the roots of an existing lawn before resowing or sodding. If you do not wish to use a chemical, then the only solution is to fork over the area and remove every single piece of the white root from the ground and dispose of it. This is just feasible in a small area, though you may have backache for several weeks. Annual weeds can be removed by this method too but in a lawn they are usually eradicated at a later stage, by regular mowing. If your ground is full of perennial grass weeds such as quack grass you must do your best to get rid of it: the quickest way is to treat it with an herbicide containing the chemical glyphosate, following the manufacturer's directions for the best results. This chemical is expensive, however, and more than one treatment may be needed, depending upon the severity of the problem.

You may simply inherit a weed-ridden plot and it will be extremely difficult to eliminate perennial weeds if they are growing among small shrubs and perennials. The only way to succeed is to be drastic and remove the plants, saving them in pots or in a clean piece of ground, making sure you remove all vestiges of weed root before transplanting. Then, having forked over the area to a good spade's depth, either fork out the roots or apply a systemic herbicide, or a combination of the two. Apply the herbicide to young green growth, following the manufacturer's directions carefully, and leave alone. Several applications or hand weeding sessions are likely to be necessary, so you must be patient. In badly infected areas you need to think in terms of a one-year eradication and renovation program.

Annual weeds in the border can be controlled by regular hoeing or hand weeding, and by mulching. Do not allow them to go to seed for, as the old saying goes, "One year's seeding, five years weeding."

Keeping the garden tidy

Keeping the garden clean and free from trash will eliminate any murky corners which tend to house pests and diseases, not to mention them looking unsightly. The removal of fallen leaves in the autumn and any leftovers in spring is a particularly necessary task in a small space. Prunings, old flowerpots, large quantities of leaves, dead flowerheads and so on all need to be removed from the site. If you bag up and remove this trash promptly, only the minimum amount of space need be left for the work/storage area. What cannot go on the compost heap (see the panel on page 100) must be disposed of at the local trash heap.

Dead-heading is a routine task during the growing season, using pruning shears to remove all the spent flowerheads and stalks, along with any diseased leaves. This will not only help extend the flowering season and retain good plant health but will also keep the garden looking tidy, which is important in a confined space where everything is continually on show. Keep your garden tools scrupulously clean to avoid spreading disease, particularly shears which have been used to remove infected material. Dip them in a disinfectant before cutting healthy plants.

Wash all containers and seed trays before use to kill off any pests and diseases and fill pots with new, sterile compost before planting. Never leave dying annuals in pots or hanging baskets at the end of the season: they look most unsightly. Empty them promptly and compost the plant material.

Regularly swept patios not only look better but are less likely to harbor algae. Gravel surfaces look cleaner and neater with regular raking over; you may wish or need to do this every spring. Paving which becomes slippery due to the buildup of green algae can be cleaned with a brand-name algicide cleaner.

Pond cleaning

The need for a complete cleanout of your pond or pool should not arise annually, and you should leave well alone as far as possible. But small pools accumulating large quantities of fallen leaves will need to be cleaned out regularly, since the decaying foliage gives off poisonous gases. In early summer, when the water is beginning to warm up and the plant life is just stirring, make a temporary shallow pool in which to keep the fish. Drain out the old water, saving any frogs, toads, newts and other creatures. Cut off the stray roots from the planted containers, and divide and replant any overgrown, starved plants, adding fertilizer pellets. Cover the aquatic plants with damp newspaper, to prevent them drying out, but aim to put them back in the water as soon as possible. Fish should ideally not be put into fresh tap water for at the least three days; this will allow some beneficial algae to develop.

Each subsequent spring, remove debris from the water and check the fish and plants over. The water can be partially changed by adding some fresh and allowing the stale to flow away, or draining out, say, half or one-third and filling with fresh water. This will eliminate some of the possible toxicity from the old water without introducing totally fresh water at a different temperature. Before starting up pumps and fountains, clean out the filters to remove any debris.

Pests and diseases

The often enclosed nature of a small garden and the specific microclimates created can encourage the proliferation of certain pests and diseases. For example, a south-facing wall in an enclosed garden will be extremely hot and dry in sunny spells, creating ideal conditions for red spider mite, so you should avoid planting climbers such as ivy, which are highly susceptible to this pest. Many roses have a propensity to diseases such as black spot and mildew and pests such as aphids and, unless you are a rose enthusiast

and do not mind using chemicals, it may be wise to avoid growing roses in quantity. The inclusion of an occasional climber or two with a good, disease-resistant health record, such as 'New Dawn,' 'Morning Jewel' or 'High Hopes,' is all I would recommend. Planting a wide diversity of plant species in your garden prevents one pest or disease readily taking hold and causing problems. Seasonal variations will also affect the range of pests or diseases most likely to appear. For example, during a spell of damp, warm weather, mildew may suddenly appear on everything, including those plants that are normally the least susceptible.

Dealing with problems

Chemical sprays are available to combat specific pests and diseases; some of these, such as the soap-based products, are more environment-friendly than others and there are sprays which will not harm beneficial insects. Insecticidal soaps will eliminate aphids if you are patient and persistent. The best time to use chemical sprays is on a still, windless day, so that spray does not drift; wear gloves and follow the manufacturer's instructions for use. Deciphering the information on a package or spray can be confusing and the following terms are often seen:

Systemic A solution that is absorbed through the surface of the leaves and translocated to all parts of the plant, including the roots. A systemic insecticide remains in the plant for a sufficient period of time to ensure that sap-sucking pests such as aphids absorb enough to be killed. With systemic herbicides, the solution remains in the plant and continues to destroy it for longer, making the result more permanent than with contact herbicides. Systemic products should be used with special care.

Contact A solution that kills the foliage, disease or pest that it touches, without traveling to the rest of the plant. It may be used to kill a wide range of pests and is useful for annual-weed control in paths.

Biological control and natural predators Picking off by hand any damaged leaves or pests to remove them, or using predators, which are beneficial insects, mites and nematodes, are the safer and preferred ways of dealing with pests. For example, vine weevil is a common pest in small gardens and

FOR THE COMPOST HEAP
- Kitchen scraps (not meat), incorporated with some garden waste
- Annual weeds (but not pernicious perennials)
- Grass clippings, mixed with more woody material or with solid waste
- Soft prunings
- Dead-headed flowers and stems
- Autumn leaves, used in moderation
- Small amounts of manure and sawdust
- Vegetable and annual crop residues

introducing a predator, along with hand removal of the weevil and grub, is the best way to deal with this problem. The predator *(Steinernema carpocapsae* or *Heterorhabditis)* can be purchased from some garden centers or through organic specialists by mail order; this live nematode is usually sold absorbed on to a sponge or clay material, then packaged in a sealed polyethylene pouch. The contents are mixed with a quantity of water, as directed, and the solution is watered on to the surface of damp soil, enabling the microscopic nematodes to "swim" to their prey. They then enter the grub's body and release bacteria which kill the grub within a few days. It should be applied only at the recommended times of year.

By avoiding sprays altogether, beneficial insects and other creatures are more likely to visit your small garden. Hoverflies and lady bugs, and their larvae in particular, eat aphids, while ground beetles, some birds, hedgehogs, frogs and toads will eat slugs and snails, an eternal pest in every garden. Butterflies, moths, bumblebees and bees will visit your garden if sufficient nectar plants are included, such as *Buddleia davidii* cultivars, *Scabiosa* 'Butterfly Blue,' *Sedum spectabile* and *Hyssopus officinalis*; these will help with the pollination of flowers. All these creatures are very sensitive to chemicals, however, including potent slug pellets. A nematode used for controlling slugs has been developed.

TEN PESTS AND DISEASES COMMON IN A SMALL GARDEN		
Pest/disease	Description/symptoms	Treatment
Aphids (greenfly and blackfly)	The small, sap-sucking insects initially appear on the new shoots of plants and excrete a sticky liquid deposit; this often becomes covered in a black, sooty mold.	Early detection prevents damage to plant growth. A small infestation can be removed by hand or by using insecticidal soaps. Use selective insecticides to avoid killing the ladybirds, hoverflies and birds which feed on aphids.
Whitefly	This sap-sucking insect generally lives on the under-surface of leaves and reduces the vigor of the plant. Usually most prevalent in a greenhouse or conservatory, it may also be a problem in a warm, sheltered space.	Regular treatment with contact and systemic sprays is required to kill all generations from adult fly to egg (see red spider mite). Because of pesticide resistance problems, the use of the parasitic wasp *Encarsia formosa* is more effective in the summer.
Red spider mite	The first signs are a mottled yellowing of the leaves followed by fine webbing, often on the under-surface of the foliage, which indicates a severe attack.	Predators can be bought to eliminate red spider mite in the conservatory or greenhouse but they are less successful outdoors. Contact sprays used on the underside of the leaf kill on contact. Systemic insecticides are even more efficient. To beat the mite's leaf cycle, treat every ten days in warm weather, alternating sprays to beat the mite's resistance.
Mealy bug	This small, gray-colored bug feeds on the sap of plants and is covered in a cotton-wool-like fluff evident on stems and leaves. It is most widely a problem on house plants but in a sheltered corner it can attack outdoors.	Touch mealy bugs with a cotton bud soaked in methylated spirits, or use a systemic insecticide; several applications may be necessary.
Leaf miners	Tiny fly larvae live between the top and bottom layers of a leaf, causing silvery tracks to appear on the foliage. Holly and chrysanthemum are particularly susceptible.	Pick off affected leaves if it is a minor attack or use a systemic insecticide.
Caterpillars	Moth or butterfly caterpillars feed on the leaves of specific plants; for example, cabbage-white caterpillars on nasturtiums. Look out for the eggs laid on the under-surface of the leaf.	Remove the caterpillars themselves by hand; rub or wash off the eggs, or spray with an insecticide; or use biological control with the bacterial spray *Bacillus thuringiensis.*
Vine weevil	The white grub or larva chews the fleshy roots, bulbs and crowns of plants and their fleshy stems; the plants will then suddenly wilt and die. The black, beetle-like adult weevil chews leaves, the telltale signs being angular-shaped holes in the edges of them. Vine weevil is often prevalent in container-grown plants.	Parasitic nematodes can be purchased and watered on to the soil around the plant to eliminate the grub. Grubs may also be found and removed when repotting. The beetle feeds at night and hides under pots and leaves by day; search for resting beetles by day and carry out evening forays with a torch for feeding weevils.
Slugs and snails	Feed on the leaves and young shoots of plants and make holes in them; young succulent growth is the most susceptible, especially of hostas. Wall shrubs and climbers provide excellent homes for snails.	Good garden hygiene is the best deterrent, avoiding damp corners where slugs and snails hibernate. Otherwise try hand picking in the early evening, or the regular application of pellets and powders not harmful to animals, or even beer can be used.
Black spot	Attacks roses; causes brown to black spots on the leaves and premature leaf fall.	Remove infected foliage and dispose of it in order not to spread the disease. Use a fungicide, following the manufacturer's instructions.
Mildew	The most likely disease in a small garden, in one of its forms, particularly on roses, vines, clematis or honeysuckle. The white powdery coating over buds and leaves (powdery mildew) is encouraged by hot, dry conditions, such as those found in the sheltered microclimate of a south-facing sun trap. Downy mildew is encouraged by damp conditions, so always avoid over-watering.	Improve air circulation. Remove the infected parts of the plant and, if necessary, use a fungicidal spray as directed.

THE YEAR IN
A SMALL GARDEN

However small your garden, the permanent backdrop will be enhanced by planting which displays seasonal characteristics.
A dark, shady corner will burst into life in early spring with the first winter aconites appearing like a ray of sunshine; colorful displays amid the scented shrubs on the patio will enhance the outdoor room in summer; and the last vestiges of autumn sunshine can stir the emotions as the soft light intensifies the rich hues of autumnal foliage. Winter gives time to pause for thought and to plan subtle changes while the evergreen foliage endures the cold and holds the structural design of your small garden together.

Repeat groupings of tulips and forget-me-nots frame the bench in this rural garden, the spring scene enhanced by the fresh greens of the surrounding countryside. Later perennials will cover the dying bulb foliage and soften the paving to paint a new picture for summer and fall. The forget-me-nots will self-seed readily for subsequent spring displays.

Winter

Winter is the season which really tests the success of your planting design. With all the deciduous trees and shrubs leafless, the outdoor scene will alter and yet the backbone planting and shaping of the garden should remain intact. As a general rule, the greater the proportion of shrubs (in particular evergreens) in the garden the more evident its winter structure will be, although this style of planting gives the least seasonal variation. By contrast, a garden with a high percentage of perennials, as in a traditional herbaceous border, will look very different in each season, but during the late autumn and winter, when the perennials have died back, there will be larger areas of bare earth.

I look upon flowers as a bonus in the winter months. What gives me great pleasure are the different shapes, textures and colors of the evergreen foliage, the different shades of brown, green, red or yellow in the bark of deciduous shrubs and the occasional over-wintering seed heads and berries. The architectural form of leafless shrubs is clearly revealed and their branches and twigs can look quite spectacular when clothed with a white hoar frost in mid-winter. A garden used and viewed daily will require a proportion of plants chosen for their interesting qualities in winter. The waft of a pleasing scent by the door or along a regularly used path will lighten the spirits on dark winter days. *Mahonia japonica*, with its lily-of-the-valley-scented flowers, and the smaller *Sarcococca hookeriana* var. *digyna* (Christmas box), whose inconspicuous flowers emit a wonderful sweet scent, both also offer good winter structure and an attractive green backdrop to summer flowers. Camellias which flower in late winter/early spring are valuable shrubs; given an acid soil and part-shade (not east-facing), they perform well as freestanding shrubs or trained on a wall (see page 98).

Snowdrops (Galanthus nivalis) *and* Skimmia reevesiana *shine out brilliantly in the subdued winter light.*

Foreground structure in the winter garden can be supplied by plants such as *Euonymus fortunei*, *E. japonica*, *Helleborus foetidus* and *H. niger*, as well as ivies and the large-leaved bergenias for ground cover. Yellow and gold foliaged plants provide good winter color; the brightness of their foliage is cheering on dull, cold days. The bright gold trifoliate leaves of *Choisya ternata* 'Sundance' adjacent to the vividly colored stems of *Cornus sanguinea* 'Winter Flame' make a wonderful plant grouping, with *Euonymus fortunei* 'Emerald 'n Gold' and *Helleborus foetidus* planted in front. To add more winter highlights, the cornus could be underplanted with clumps of snowdrops.

A well-planned and well-planted small garden requires a minimal amount of time in the winter, doing the occasional tidying, protecting or preparing for spring. Yet on a cold but sunny day it can be enormously pleasurable to wrap up and set to work in the garden, tackling a few of the tasks from the checklist.

- Ensure that all plants in pots have enough water, especially if they are under the overhang of a building. Also make sure they are sufficiently well drained—stand them on pot feet—to prevent the pot cracking in prolonged freezing conditions. Protect susceptible pots and plants, such as *Cistus*, hardy fuchsias and *Pittosporum*, with bubble plastic or burlap.
- Protect plants that are only moderately hardy, such as *Clematis cirrhosa balearica* and *Fremontodendron californicum*, with bracken, newspaper, burlap or a frost blanket.
- Conifers with an upright habit of growth are particularly susceptible to snow damage; it is advisable to tie them up in early winter by pulling the branches together with string.
- Continue moving plants or planting shrubs provided conditions are not too wet or frozen.
- Prune roses and fruit trees after the danger of frost has passed (see page 94).
- Prune wisteria to encourage flowering spurs by cutting lateral shoots that were pruned last summer to within six or seven leaf joints from the main stem (see page 97).
- Repair any broken garden tools and have the lawn mower serviced and the blades sharpened.
- Retain a small ice-free hole in ponds stocked with fish to allow the toxic gases to escape. Melt the ice by holding a pan of boiling water on it or using a pool heater; never smash a hole in the ice as the fish suffer severe shock.
- After any heavy snowfalls, knock the snow off tree branches and other plants.
- A dry winter day is an ideal time to treat woodwork with non-toxic preservative, when it is most accessible and the foliage of deciduous plants cannot be damaged. Cover evergreen plants or tie them back out of the way.
- Finish carrying out repairs to fences, trellis and other climbing supports (see page 98).
- Clean metal or plastic garden furniture and oil wooden furniture to prolong its life.
- Keep paved areas clean by sweeping.

Spring

Spring is a time of anticipation—it means that warmer weather is on the way and life stirs even in the smallest garden. The colorful range of spring bulbs starts off the season, with early narcissi, crocuses and grape hyacinths appearing under deciduous shrubs and in the spaces later to be filled with the foliage of perennial plants. The bright greens of newly unfurling leaves, alongside those of the evergreens that have retained their shine through the winter, tone well with the bright yellow and blue flower colors predominating in spring.

Before the dense foliage canopy of deciduous trees and large shrubs excludes light from the ground beneath them, spring flowers have their chance of a starring role. The clear blue flowers of *Pulmonaria angustifolia* 'Munstead Blue' associate well with bright yellow narcissi and the purple foliage hues of the ground-covering *Ajuga reptans* 'Braunherz.' *Euphorbia robbiae* is one of my spring favorites for planting in a very dry, sunny or shady spot where nothing else will succeed. Its abundant lime-green flowers last for many weeks before fading.

The weather can still be cruel at this time of year, however, and warmer days are often interspersed with cold, frosty spells. Spring frosts are the most damaging since rising temperatures and longer days encourage new, tender growth which is then extremely susceptible to frost damage. Be prepared to wrap the more tender, early starters in a frost blanket if frosts or snow are forecast. Some tender shrubs and climbers may still need winter protection during these cold spells.

Space and time permitting, spring is the season to prepare, to sow, to pot and plant subjects for summer color. Once the danger of frost is past, plant some tubs with bedding material to enliven the patio or to brighten a corner of the garden (see page 83).

The bright spring foliage of the evergreen Elaeagnus ebbingei *'Limelight' sets off the* Narcissus *'February Gold.'*

- Prune late-flowering summer shrubs such as hardy fuchsias, as well as late-flowering clematis (see page 94). Prune hard, to ground level, shrubs that are grown for their foliage like dogwoods, variegated elders and *Acer negundo* 'Flamingo.'
- Train in the new growth of climbers, especially clematis, as it appears (see page 98), to retain a neat plant, spreading within bounds.
- Young, tender shoots and seedlings are susceptible to slug and snail damage. Watch for evidence, before it is too late, and remove the offenders either by hand or with slug bait that is harmless to other creatures (see page 101).
- Apply a thick mulch of bulky organic matter, and rake in a top-dressing of organic fertilizer such as bonemeal, around established shrubs and herbaceous plants (see page 91).
- Tidy any debris from under the hedge and apply a spring fertilizer.
- Spike lawns for aeration and apply a moss killer, before feeding them (see page 92).

- Top-dress permanently planted pots by removing the top 2 to 3 in. of compost and replacing it with appropriate new compost, adding a balanced-nutrient fertilizer.
- Give ivies a spring-clean by clipping off damaged foliage and brushing them down to remove any dead leaves.
- Trim winter heathers with shears when they have finished flowering to remove the flowered growth and encourage a compact habit.
- Complete the planting out of shrubs during mild spells.
- Divide snowdrops just after flowering, when they are still in leaf; dig up a clump and replant the bulbs in small groups elsewhere.
- Divide large established clumps of perennials to retain heathly growth. Replant the divisions in small groups at approximately 1½ to 2 ft. intervals, where needed.
- Check that you have sufficient pots, labels and potting compost ready for the busiest season in the garden.
- Plant lily bulbs in well-drained soil or in fresh compost in containers (see page 83).
- To provide late summer scent, sow seed of annuals such as night-scented stock (*Matthiola bicornis*) and *Nicotiana* directly into pots or in the ground once the soil starts to warm up.
- Clean empty window boxes and containers ready for the new season. Once the spring container displays are past their best, empty out the pots and replant them with summer flowers. Be careful not to plant half-hardy and tender subjects too early, in case you lose them with a late frost.
- Mulch pots and borders with coconut shells, fine bark or gravel, to help retain moisture.
- Cut a few stems of flowering shrubs such as *Jasminum nudiflorum* or *Forsythia* in bud and bring them into the house to enjoy an early flower display.
- Repair any joints in paving and re-lay uneven slabs (do not do this on a frosty day).

Summer

This is the season when you can enjoy the fruits of your labors. You can sit in the garden, surrounded by the heady scents of summer jasmine (*Jasminum officinale*) clothing the nearby wooden arbor. Trees and shrubs will be in full leaf, casting shade and creating patterns where dappled light falls through their delicate foliage canopies. The sun is high in the sky and sunlight at its brightest, strengthening hot colors while slightly fading the softer shades. The contrasts of sun and shade will provide different atmospheres within the garden.

The spring-flowering shrubs will be fading, making way for the next burst of color provided by the herbaceous perennials and summer-flowering shrubs. The compact habit of *Philadelphus* 'Manteau d'Hermine,' with its plentiful creamy-white scented flowers, makes it the most suitable mock orange for the small garden while the slightly more tender *Cistus* and *Hebe*, needing full sun, will flower profusely throughout summer in a range of colors from whites to pinks to lilac and blue shades. *Hebe* 'Autumn Glory' with its deep purple-blue flowers and dark purple-green, round leaves provides interest from early summer to late autumn. The single, flat flowers of *Cistus*, lasting one day only, are followed by new buds opening in rapid succession. The compact forms of *C.* 'Silver Pink,' with silver pink flowers and gray foliage, and *C. pulverulentus* 'Sunset,' with deep cerise-pink flowers and gray leaves, fit well into a sunny border. Adjacent plantings of pale yellow flowers such as those of *Hemerocallis* 'Whichford' and *Verbascum* 'Gainsborough' would echo the yellow centers of the pink cistus flowers. Plum-colored background foliage of *Berberis thunbergii* 'Lombart's Purple,' or the rich purple leaves of *Heuchera micrantha* 'Palace Purple' in the foreground, would set off the pale pink flowers of *C. pulverulentus* 'Sunset.'

Actinidia kolomikta, Geranium psilostemon *and* Clematis 'Hagley Hybrid' *complement each other and the brick wall in high summer.*

Pockets of abundant high-summer flower color among the shrubs would be provided by *Diascia*, *Geranium*, the blue-flowered *Nepeta* (ideal for edging borders), *Campanula* and the ever-reliable *Alchemilla mollis*. By late summer hydrangeas, fuchsias, late-flowering clematis and many of the daisy-flowered perennials will have burst into full bloom.

• The sheltered environment of many small gardens, particularly those in full sun, will cause the soil to dry out very quickly. Unless you have selected drought-tolerant species for hot borders, you will have to water regularly during the summer months.
• You will need to water sun-baked pots and hanging baskets up to twice a day. Place potted plant displays out of the midday sun if regular watering is not possible. Give one thorough soaking rather than regular little sprays.
• Feed your hanging baskets and tubs regularly with fertilizer (see page 91); a food with a

high level of potash is best for flowering plants. After cutting back spring- and early-summer-flowering perennials, feed them and you may well get a second crop of flowers.
• Dead-head all flowering plants regularly to encourage maximum length of flowering period and to keep the garden tidy (see page 99).
• In late summer, prune the wispy tendrils of wisteria (see page 97).
• Keep a watchful eye out for indications of pests and diseases on your plants and take the necessary action to control (see page 101).
• Maintain a weekly mowing regime for your lawn, cutting it to ½ in. or 1 in. high (see page 92).
• A well-used small lawn may have some bare patches and early summer is the time to reseed these areas (see page 92).
• Clip hedges to maintain their shape and size (see page 97).
• Consider the installation of low-voltage lighting while you are using the garden (see page 62). You could perhaps highlight a focal point or favorite specimen plant to draw the garden into the house when it is not warm enough to be outside, creating an evening picture for all seasons. (The actual installation of any lighting in an established garden is best done in autumn, when there is least disruption to plants.)

Autumn

At the end of the growing season the late-summer sunshine casts a glow over the garden. The leaves of *Acer*, *Cotinus* and *Amelanchier* radiate their autumn colors and become almost translucent as the sun shines through them. You might decide to plant an ornamental maple, such as *Acer palmatum* or *A. senkaki*, or even a *Cotinus*, where its foliage will catch the evening sun shining from behind, to give this magical quality to the autumn scene.

The warm, russet tones harmonize well with many of the compact, autumn-flowering shrubs and perennials suitable for the smaller garden. The violet-blue, bead-like flower spikes of *Liriope muscari* appear from among the clumps of dark evergreen leaves to give weeks of late color; this plant is ideal for dry places among shrubs. *Dianthus*, *Persicaria*, *Sedum*, *Schizostylis*, *Hebe* and *Potentilla* will all provide autumn interest. Even in the smallest space, it is worth making room for a bold group of late-flowering perennials such as *Aster*, *Helenium* or *Rudbeckia*. Their flowers, in shades of deep brick red, orange, dark red and deep yellow, look stunning in association with autumn foliage. At the front of the border, the heart-shaped leaves of *Heuchera micrantha* 'Palace Purple' become a translucent bronze-red, the foliage of *Euphorbia polychroma* 'Purpurea' also intensifies in color and the small spiraeas such as *Spiraea × bumalda* 'Gold Flame' gain attractive autumn hues.

To offset your collection of plants for autumn highlights, plant evergreen shrubs with gold foliage or, in acid soil, a group of golden foliaged heathers or, at the back of the border, the larger *Ilex aquifolium* 'Golden King' with its almost thornless gold-variegated leaves. Fuchsias and hydrangeas are both happy in light shade and can be used in a part of the garden where the sun now only reaches for a short while as it gets lower in the sky. *Hydrangea* 'Preziosa,' with deep pink flowers, or one of the white lacecap hydrangeas are my favorites for the smaller garden. In mild or sheltered plots, the hardy fuchsias may well remain evergreen. The delicate white-tinged pink flowers of *Fuchsia magellanica* var. *molinae* hang gracefully amid their bright green foliage and associate well with the large gray leaves of *Hosta sieboldiana* 'Elegans' and *H.* 'Halcyon.'

Walls and fences can look stunning at this time of year. Evergreen climbers and wall shrubs such as *Pyracantha* and *Cotoneaster*

The evergreen Mahonia japonica *dons its fall russet tones, which last well into winter, when it produces its yellow flowers.*

display a range of colored berries in shades from yellow to orange and red. These will attract the birds as the temperature drops and food becomes more scarce. I love to see the dying flowerheads of climbing hydrangea (*Hydrangea anomala petiolaris*) aging to pink and finally brown, covered in cobwebs on a damp, misty autumn morning. But the most spectacular sight provided by autumn climbers has to be that of Virginia creeper (*Parthenocissus quinquefolia*). The dramatic vivid orange-red or even plum-red colors of the foliage before it falls last for a very short time but can totally transform a large boundary wall.

- As a general rule, you should prune deciduous flowering shrubs which flower on the current year's growth in late autumn to early spring (see page 94).
- Autumn is the time to scarify, spike and hollow-tine the lawn (see page 92).
- New gardens and newly created borders

should ideally be dug over at this time, especially on heavy soil, before the ground becomes too waterlogged.

- Divide or move overgrown, established clumps of herbaceous plants now. Lift them carefully, retaining as much root as possible.
- While the soil is still warm and moist, plant new shrubs to encourage good root growth before winter sets in. Wait for a mild spell or cover the area you wish to plant with organic matter or a mulch material to keep it workable in frosty spells. Never plant into frozen ground.
- A wide range of specimen trees and shrubs are available during the latter part of autumn and winter; you will find that trees supplied bare-rooted are often less expensive than their container-grown counterparts.
- Check that boundary fences, trellis and other plant supports are sound and able to cope with the weight of the climbers on them, even in a gale. Replace any unstable or rotten fence posts early in the season.
- Plant spring-flowering bulbs in the early autumn for both the garden and for pots. Use a well-drained compost in containers and mix the bulbs with winter bedding and evergreen shrubs for effective displays. Try a mixture of *Tulipa* 'Apricot Beauty' with pale blue Universal pansies and silver-variegated ivies to trail over the side of the containers.
- Clear away fallen leaves from the lawn, from around small plants and especially from the patio where they may make it very slippery. Allow some fallen leaves to remain around shrubs for overwintering beneficial insects or other hibernating animals.
- If space permits, store the leaves in plastic bags to make leaf mold (this will take up to two years to rot down completely, before using it on the garden).
- Remove any fallen leaves from the pond before they sink to the bottom and start to decay. Net the pond if necessary.

KEY PLANTS FOR THE SMALL GARDEN

The fifty plants included here have been selected for their contribution to the overall display in a small garden; most of them are widely available. A proportion of the key plants are evergreen, giving the garden year-round structure, while others bring valuable seasonal variations and highlights. Cultivars are recommended either for their neat habit of growth, long-flowering attributes, their scent or their seasonal interest. The shrubs and climbers chosen all respond well to pruning, which will be essential in order to retain the balance of the composition over the years.

Every plant must contribute to the overall display within a small space, but the successful association of plants within a group brings a further dimension to the planting design. The bright yellow-green flowers of Alchemilla mollis here enhance the deep yellow centers of this tiny cream viola. Nature's own combination of the scalloped leaves of Alchemilla with its delicate lime-green flowers is especially effective.

Specimen trees

Acer
Maple

This genus contains a large range of trees and shrubs but the following two species are particularly suitable for a small garden in terms of their all-round interest. *Acer davidii*, the snake-barked maple, makes an ideal specimen tree, grown mainly for its glossy purple-green and white striated bark, displayed at its best in winter. During summer the spreading head of rich green leaves are borne on rhubarb-red branches. It has good yellow autumn color. The paperbark maple, *A. griseum*, displays cinnamon-colored peeling bark in winter and vivid scarlet and flame autumn foliage.

Size H: 13–20 ft.; S: 10–13 ft. **Aspect** Full sun to light shade. **Hardiness** Hardy. **Soil** Thrives best in acid soil. **After-care** Best left to grow naturally; young shoots can be pruned to reduce overall size. **Planting partners** *Polystichum setiferum* Divisilobum group, *Brachyglottis* 'Sunshine,' *Dicentra spectabilis* 'Alba.'

Gleditsia triacanthos 'Sunburst'

Amelanchier canadensis
Snowy mespilus

The racemes of white flowers produced in late spring are soon followed by the unfurling ovate delicate foliage with a coppery hue. As summer approaches the leaves turn to light green and have a slight orange-red veining. In autumn the foliage turns brilliant red-orange and small light red fruits may be produced (depending on the heat and dryness of the summer). It may be grown as a standard tree or purchased and grown as a multi-stemmed bush.

Size H: 20–23 ft.; S: 15½–20 ft. **Hardiness** Hardy. **Soil** Any garden soil, acid or alkaline. **After-care** No regular pruning required, but may be cut back hard, with its lower branches removed, or trimmed and shaped in winter to retain it. **Planting partners** *Ilex aquifolium* 'Golden Queen,' *Heuchera* 'Pewter Moon,' *Liriope muscari*.

Apple see *Malus*

Autumn-flowering cherry see *Prunus × subhirtella* 'Fallalis'

Gleditsia triacanthos
Honey locust

A very slow-growing form of *Gleditsia triacanthos*, 'Rubylace' has a light canopy of ruby-red fern-like foliage darkening to bronze-green as the leaves mature. *G. triacanthos* 'Sunburst' is equally attractive but has beautiful bright yellow-green pinnate leaves and is more vigorous in habit, reaching one-third more in size. Both have brittle branches which may be subject to wind damage.

Size H: 15½–20 ft.; S: 6½ ft. **Aspect** Full sun to light shade. **Hardiness** Hardy, tolerates atmospheric pollution. **Soil** Any well-drained soil. **After-care** Shorten the previous season's growth in spring to improve overall shape while young. **Planting partners** with 'Rubylace': *Anemone hupehensis* 'September Charm'; with 'Sunburst': *Campanula lactiflora*, *Berberis thunbergii* 'Rose Glow.'

Honey locust see *Gleditsia triacanthos*

Malus
Apple

Those who would like their small tree to provide as well as be decorative might include a culinary apple tree. Purchase a reliable cultivar of *Malus domestica* on a dwarfing rootstock so that it does not grow too large and overshadow all else. 'Golden Delicious' is a reliable cropper and has a good health record; 'Jon-A-Red' produces fruit with an outstanding flavor and is a most reliable cropper; both these will pollinate themselves as well as other varieties. These cultivars can also be fan-trained along a sheltered wall or trained over a tunnel or arch.

Some ornamental flowering and crab apples are also available budded onto dwarfing rootstock. Desirable disease-resistant ornamental crab apples include 'Amberina' (red fruit, white flowers), 'Donald Wyman' (red fruits, white-pink flowers), 'Ormiston Roy' (yellow fruits, white flowers), 'Royalty' (crimson flowers, red fruits) and the weeping cultivars 'Red Swan,' 'Coral Cascade' and 'Red Jade.'

Malus domestica on dwarfing rootstock: **Size** H: 6 ft.; S: Plant bushes 4 ft. apart, cordons 2 ft. apart. **Aspect** An open site with plenty of sun. **Hardiness** Hardy; avoid frost pockets to prevent damage to spring blossom. **Soil** A well-prepared fertile soil. **After-care** Train to desired shape by pruning in autumn and early spring. **Planting partners** *Helenium* 'Moerheim Beauty,' *Humulus lupulus* 'Aureus,' *Rosa* 'Graham Thomas.'

Malus 'Evereste': **Size** H: 10 ft.; S: 6½ ft. **Aspect** Prefers full sun, but tolerates light shade. **Hardiness** Hardy. **Soil** Any garden soil, except waterlogged. **After-care** Prune straggly specimens hard immediately after flowering. **Planting partners** *Epimedium × rubrum*, *Hosta* 'Francee.'

Maple see *Acer*

Prunus × subhirtella
'Fallalis'
Autumn flowering cherry

This delightful tree has a light, round-topped canopy of foliage in summer and yellow autumn color, followed by small white flowers opening on the bare twigs in mild spells from early to late winter. It is delicate, casts dappled shade and is never overbearing in a confined space. 'Fallalis Rosea' has

rosy pink flowers and the slower, smaller-growing 'Fukubana' has enchanting semi-double, rose-madder flowers in early spring. All are good for flower arranging.

Size H and S: 16–23 ft. **Aspect** Prefers full sun but tolerates light shade. **Hardiness** Hardy. **Soil** Any garden soil. **After-care** No pruning required; shape if necessary. **Planting partners** *Galanthus nivalis* 'Flore Pleno,' *Hedera helix helix*.

Purple osier see
Salix purpurea 'Pendula'

Salix purpurea 'Pendula'
Purple osier

This small-growing, weeping member of the willow family associates well with water. The purple to purple-green, long pendulous bare branches are attractive in winter before they become covered by the narrow, gray-purple foliage which turns yellow in autumn. Yellow catkins are produced in spring before the leaves appear. Do not plant near to drains, as the roots of this tree seek out water.

Size H and S: 10 ft. **Aspect** Full sun. **Hardiness** Hardy. **Soil** Prefers a moist soil. **After-care** Reduce in size in spring to retain within its allotted space. **Planting partners** *Alchemilla mollis*, *Miscanthus sinensis* 'Strictus,' *Rodgersia podophylla*.

Snowy mespilus see
Amelanchier canadensis

Sorbus vilmorinii

The choice of a tree is a crucial part of the design for a small garden. The slow-growing species included will take several years to attain their ultimate height.

Sorbus vilmorinii

Several seasons of interest are produced from this one small tree. The elegant canopy of purple-green foliage with a gray sheen complements a rose-pink and silver planting scheme. As autumn approaches, the foliage turns red and purple and the characteristic drooping clusters of fruits are red at first, gradually changing to pink.

Size H: 16 ft.; S: 8 ft. **Aspect** Full sun to light shade. **Hardiness** Hardy. **Soil** Any garden soil. **After-care** No pruning required. **Planting partners** *Liriope muscari*, *Euphorbia characias wulfenii*.

Background and structural plants

Clematis 'Rouge
Cardinal'

Cherry laurel see
Prunus laurocerasus

Choisya ternata

Mexican orange blossom

This shrub has a compact, round, shapely form. Its bright green glossy foliage will lighten an otherwise dull corner and form a pleasing backdrop to the more ephemeral perennials. It may be fan-trained on to a wall or trellis. The trifoliate leaves emit a pungent aroma when crushed and the white flowers, appearing from spring to early summer, are orange-scented. The yellow-leaved 'Sundance' works well in a gold and green scheme; it is slightly less hardy than the species, does better in sun and is smaller.

Size H and S: 6½ ft. **Aspect** Full sun to deep shade. **Hardiness** Hardy, but cold winds in a severe winter can cause damage. **Soil** Most garden soils, though severe alkalinity may cause chlorosis. **After-care** Light pruning in early summer encourages spasmodic flowering; on mature shrubs, remove one-third of the oldest wood to ground level after flowering to encourage rejuvenation from center and base. **Planting partners** *Asperula odorata*, *Tiarella cordifolia*, *Iris foetidissima* 'Variegata.'

Clematis

(large-flowered hybrids)

Clematis are almost essential in every small garden. I have selected hybrids and cultivars which combine a compact habit of growth with a vigorous growing record and a long flowering season. Those listed below flower from early to late summer, with a short break in between, except those with an asterisk (*) which flower once, from mid- to late summer. 'Alice Fisk': extremely compact wisteria-blue flowers with a crenulated edge and brown stamens; 'Asao': cartwheels of reddish-pink sepals with a white bar; 'Barbara Jackman': large blue/mauve flowers with a carmine bar, shade will enhance the color of the bar; 'Dawn': tidy habit, very large, pearly pink flowers, ideal in a shady spot; 'Doctor Ruppel': rose-red sepals with a carmine bar and gold anthers, 'Edith'*: large, white sepals with pretty red/brown anthers; 'Hagley Hybrid'* excellent in a tub, shell-pink petals with darker stamens (avoid full sun or the flowers will fade); 'Rouge Cardinal'*: velvety, glowing crimson square-tipped sepals and yellow stamens; 'The President'*: velvety blue-purple flowers with a paler stripe, anthers red/purple.

Size H: 6–8 ft.; S: Indefinite but prune to control. **Aspect** Any. **Hardiness** Hardy, but the roots should be protected from hot sun. **Soil** Any garden soil but preferably rich and well fed; use a soil-based potting compost in tubs. **After-care** These clematis do not need annual pruning; just remove weak and dead growth. To confine their spread, cut back in early spring; the early flowers will be lost after pruning. Mulch in the autumn and apply a small handful of sulfate of potash in spring. Feed generously during the growing season, giving a weekly dose of high-potash liquid fertilizer between the first and second crop of flowers. **Planting partners** Allow to grow through roses and evergreen shrubs.

Clematis cirrhosa balearica

The delicate ferny evergreen foliage of this clematis will ramble over shrubs or up a trellis in a sheltered aspect. Pendant, scented, cup-shaped creamy flowers, spotted purple inside, appear during winter in mild spells, set against the evergreen foliage which has purple/bronze winter hues. The silky seed heads are a summer feature.

Size H and S: 8 ft. **Aspect** Needs shelter from cold winds; roots need shade. **Hardiness** Moderately hardy but will suffer in a prolonged cold spell. **Soil** Tolerates acid and alkaline soils. **After-care** Remove any dead or weak stems. Flowers on growth made the previous year. If outgrowing its situation, cut back after flowering; severe pruning results in fewer flowers next year. **Planting partners** *Helleborus orientalis*, *H. niger*, *Galanthus nivalis*, *Euonymus fortunei* 'Silver Queen.'

Elaeagnus

This group of shrubs gives excellent backdrop year-round foliage which lasts well indoors; it is fairly drought-resistant. Insignificant silvery white flowers, appearing in winter, are sometimes scented. *E. × ebbingei* 'Lime-light,' with central gold splashes on the leaves, and *E. × ebbingei* 'Gilt Edge,' with gold margins, are both quick-growing. In an exposed site, try the slightly more hardy *E. pungens* 'Maculata,' whose dark, ovate leaves have central gold patches. *E. pungens* 'Dicksonii' is less vigorous in habit and therefore suited to very small gardens. **Size** H and S: 6½ ft. **Aspect** Full sun to dappled shade. **Hardiness** Hardy, but may require some protection from cold winds. **Soil** Most garden soils, except extremely alkaline or dry. **After-care** Trim in late winter/early spring; may be pruned hard if needed. **Planting partners** *Clematis macropetala*, *Lonicera nitida* 'Baggesen's Gold,' *Viola* 'Clementina.'

Garrya elliptica

Silk tassel bush

This evergreen wall shrub produces magnificent long, silver-gray catkins up to 12 in. long in mild winters; its dark, shiny rounded leaves have woolly undersides. The shrub protrudes up to 3 ft. The male form of the cultivar 'James Roof' has longer, shinier catkins. Good for coastal areas and shady gardens.
Size H: 11½ ft.; S: 8 ft. **Aspect** Shade; avoid exposed sites as bitter spring winds can damage the foliage. **Hardiness** Hardy. **Soil** Any garden

soil. **After-care** Train along a wall; in spring, shorten back any side-branches not needed for the framework to within 2 in. **Planting partners** *Hedera helix helix* 'Goldchild,' *Clematis* 'Minuet,' ferns.

Hedera helix helix

Ivy

Ivies are one of the most useful plants for vertical cover, ground cover and for evergreen structure in pots and hanging baskets. The pads, which cling to the wall, are for support only and will not eat into brick walls or fences. Regular maintenance will prevent them from growing excessively large. Avoid a hot, dry situation where red spider mite is likely to thrive.

My preference is for the smaller-leaved cultivars, which have a compact habit of growth and make an excellent backdrop. Recommended cultivars include: 'Buttercup,' 'Angularis Aurea' and 'Mrs Pollock': their golden variegated foliage combines well with yellow and blue planting schemes or red/orange autumn foliage and berries; 'Glacier,' 'Cavendishii,' 'Eva,' 'Tess' and 'Sagittifolia Variegata': their silver variegated leaves associate well with gray foliage and with pale pink to cerise flowers; 'Succinata,' 'Pedata' and 'Glymii': interestingly shaped green leaves; 'Succinata' adopts hues of amber-green in full sun. Silver/cream variegated 'Adam,' 'Eva' and 'Glacier' are useful for ground cover and for containers. For shady ground cover and pots the best green-leaved cultivars are 'Shamrock' and 'Fleur de Lis.'
Size H and S: Unlimited. **Aspect** Sun

Clematis cirrhosa balearica

This group of plants is essential for clothing walls, fences and structures and providing a few strong statements in your outdoor room, as well as furnishing a backdrop to the more decorative planting.

to full shade; variegated cultivars tend to lose their variegation in shade, except 'Sagittifolia Variegata' and 'Buttercup.' **Hardiness** Very hardy. **Soil** Any garden soil. **After-care** Reduce in size by pruning in mid-spring; may be cut back to ground level and will regenerate from the base. At the end of winter clip off any growth which threatens to become invasive and tidy by removing browning leaves. Look out for red spider mite in hot weather and for mealy bug. **Planting partners** *Parthenocissus tricuspidata* 'Veitchii,' *Clematis*.

Holly see *Ilex*

Hydrangea anomala petiolaris

Climbing hydrangea

This deciduous climber has a self-clinging habit and light green, finely toothed foliage turning yellow in autumn. Its copious white lace-cap flowers, borne from midsummer on, fade to pink then turn brown in late autumn. It is slow-growing to start but, once established, the peeling brown bark·and remains of flowerheads soften a shady wall even in winter.
Size H and S: 13–20 ft. **Aspect** Any, but does well in shade. **Hardiness** Hardy. **Soil** Any garden soil, providing plenty of moisture to establish. **After-care** No pruning required but shorten the spurs immediately after

Hydrangea anomala petiolaris

flowering. At first, new shoots may need to be anchored to their support. **Planting partners** *Clematis alpina*, *Hosta* 'Marginata Alba,' *Prunus laurocerasus* 'Variegata.'

Firethorn see *Pyracantha*

Ilex

Holly

This genus includes a wide range of indispensable evergreen shrubs and trees which are generally slow-growing and very receptive to training, whether as a hedge, ball, tier, spiral or regularly clipped freestanding shrub in the border. The hardy *Ilex aquifolium* is parent to many of the decorative forms useful in a small garden. *Ilex × altaclarensis* 'Golden King,' with its almost spineless, shiny, round leaves with broad yellow-gold margins, is a female form and berries freely in autumn if pollinated by a male form such as *I. aquifolium* 'Silver Queen,' which has creamy white margins to its dark green leaves; the berrying silver-variegated *I. aquifolium* 'Handsworth New Silver' has creamy-white-margined leaves; the green-leaved *I. aquifolium* 'J.C. van Tol' will berry without a partner.
Size H: 13 ft.; S: 8 ft. if unclipped. **Aspect** Any, but useful for shade. **Hardiness** Hardy. **Soil** Any garden soil. **After-care** May be reduced in size or simply trimmed in early spring. **Planting partners** with gold forms: *Parthenocissus tricuspidata* 'Veitchii'; *Amelanchier canadensis*; with silver forms: *Rosmarinus officinalis*, *Clematis* 'Niobe.'

Mexican orange blossom see *Choisya ternata*

Ivy see *Hedera helix helix*

Laurustinus see *Viburnum tinus*

Prunus laurocerasus

Cherry laurel

The cherry laurel may seem very ordinary but, when regularly clipped and managed, its bright, glossy, evergreen leaves create an excellent backdrop or screen when grown as a specimen or a hedge and it can be clipped to topiary shapes. 'Schipkaensis' has narrower, dark green leaves and is slightly less vigorous; 'Zabeliana,' with an obliquely branched, spreading habit reaches only 3–3 ft. 3 in. in height by 10–16 ft. in spread. The silver-variegated 'Variegata' is a slow-growing goblet-shaped shrub which reaches up to 6½ ft.
Size H and S: 20 ft. if left unclipped. **Aspect** Any, but especially useful in shade. **Hardiness** Hardy. **Soil** Any, except extremely alkaline. **After-care** Prune in late winter/early spring to control its size; reduced to ground level it will rejuvenate quickly. **Planting partners** *Euonymus fortunei* 'Emerald 'n Gold,' *Ilex × altaclarensis* 'Golden King.'

Pyracantha

Firethorn

A group of robust and versatile evergreens, thriving in most situations and ideal for fan-training on vertical supports. Formal training will create hori-

zontal tiers of growth, while regular pruning will develop a less precise look, and clipping hard will minimize the forward spread. Hawthorn-like flowers with a musty scent are borne in mid-summer and in autumn/winter abundant clusters of berries in shades of red, orange and yellow cover the dark green, ovate folige. The berries (yellow ones tend to remain longer) will attract winter-feeding birds. Long, sharp spines in the leaf axils make this an unpleasant shrub to prune. Suggested cultivars include: 'Harlequin' with silver/white edged foliage and small orange-red fruit; 'Soleil d'Or' with deep yellow fruit; 'Orange Glow' with freely produced orange fruit; 'Red Cushion,' a more compact form (up to 3 ft. 3 in. high) with red berries.
Size H: 10 ft.; S: 6½ ft. Aspect Any. Hardiness Very hardy. Soil Any garden soil, but avoid extreme alkalinity. After-care Trim and shape as desired in late summer, cutting back the current year's growth to reveal the ripening berries. Additional pruning may be required to keep it within bounds. Planting partners *Forsythia × intermedia* 'Lynwood,' *Rhamnus alaternus* 'Argenteovariegatus.'

___

Rhamnus alaternus
'Argenteovariegatus'
Variegated buckthorn

A silver-variegated evergreen shrub, especially good in coastal districts. Whether grown fan-trained or freestanding, it forms a good backdrop to pink, wine-red, white and silver plant groupings. The masses of tiny leaves contrast well with bold foliage.
Size H: 10–13 ft.; S: 6½–10 ft., unclipped. Aspect Sun or semi-shade. Hardiness Slightly tender; needs some protection from cold winds. Soil Any garden soil, except extremely wet. After-care Prune in late spring once established. Planting partners *Choisya ternata*, *Juniperus communis* 'Repanda,' *Chaenomeles × superba* 'Pink Lady.'

___

Ribes laurifolium
Winter-flowering currant

The narrow, elliptical glabrous leaves of this unusual shrub are displayed to best effect in a small space when the plant is fan-trained on a sheltered wall or fence. Clematis growing through this backdrop foliage will provide summer color, while in late winter/early spring small racemes of pendulous greenish-white male flowers are produced in the leaf axils of established plants.
Size H: 5–6 ft.; S: 3–6 ft. Aspect Full sun to light shade; requires shelter. Hardiness Hardy. Soil Most garden soils. After-care Train to a fan shape on a wall or fence. Planting partners *Clematis* 'Dawn,' *Hedera helix helix* 'Eva,' *Helleborus foetidus*.

___

Rosa
Climbing roses

For a small garden the best choice is a rose of compact habit with good foliage health and a long flowering season. The pale pink 'New Dawn'* is ideal for a pergola, trellis or wall; 'High Hopes'* is a warm, light rose-

Rosa 'Compassion'

pink, strongly perfumed, flowering later in the season with an outstanding health record; 'Morning Jewel'* has bright pink flowers and will grow on any aspect; 'Compassion' is salmon-pink and apricot, sweetly scented; 'Sympathie'* has bright, blood-red flowers and will grow over 15 ft. tall; 'Dublin Bay'* is a similar color but more compact and flowers well into autumn; 'Highfield' is one of the most healthy yellows and has a lovely scent; 'White Cockade' bears its shapely, scented white blooms on a compact plant.
Size H: 10–12 ft. Aspect Generally full sun; those (above) marked with an asterisk (*) will tolerate some shade but tend to become leggy. Hardiness Hardy. Soil Prefer a rich, heavy soil. After-care. Mulch with organic matter in autumn, prune in early spring and feed (with a rose fertilizer) and water regularly during the growing season to ensure strong growth. Dead-head as the blooms fade. Planting partners *Clematis*.

Silk tassel bush see *Garrya elliptica*

Taxus baccata
Yew

The English yew will grow to enormous proportions but, when regularly trimmed, provides an excellent formal hedge which can be kept as narrow as 18 in. Several cultivars may be even more useful in a small plot: 'Fastigiata' and 'Fastigiata Aurea' have a narrow, columnar habit making them both useful as vertical accent plants in a confined space. 'Repandens' is a slow-growing, semi-prostrate form, whose drooping tips hang gracefully over the edge of a raised bed; the linear, almost black-green leaves make a useful foil to lighter flowers and contrast well with bold leaf shapes.

Taxus baccata 'Repandens': **Size** H: 12–20 in.; S: 5–6½ ft. **Aspect** Any. **Hardiness** Hardy. **Soil** Any garden soil. **After-care** Trim to retain the shape and size required. **Planting partners** *Bergenia stracheyi alba, Aucuba japonica* 'Crotonifolia,' *Saxifraga × urbium, Vinca minor* 'Variegata.'

Variegated buckthorn
see ***Rhamnus alaternus***
'Argenteovariegatus'

Viburnum tinus
Laurustinus

This evergreen shrub, ideal as a backdrop, can be grown either freestanding or fan-trained, especially on a north-facing wall or fence. The broad, ovate dark green leaves with lighter silver undersides provide an effective foil to the small to medium clusters of pinky white tubular flowers, opening in spring from deep pink buds carried through the winter. *V. tinus* 'Variegatum' is a more compact-growing form, slightly less winter-hardy and reaching two-thirds the size of the species; it has white flowers and creamy-white variegated foliage which contrast well with dark green leaved shrubs.

Size H and S: 6½ ft. **Aspect** Full sun to medium shade. **Hardiness** Hardy.

Soil Any garden soil. **After-care** Trim to the desired shape and size after flowering; it responds well to clipping. On shrubs more than 5 years old, remove one-third of the oldest wood down to ground level in early spring to encourage rejuvenation from the base. **Planting partners** *Ilex aquifolium* 'Argentea Marginata,' *Rhamnus alaternus* 'Argenteovariegatus.'

Weigela florida
'Albovariegata'

Creamy white edges to the ovate leaves and an upright, compact, bushy growth habit make this a useful summer foliage shrub, with pale pink, lightly scented flowers in midsummer. It can be trained as a wall shrub if space is restricted; it can also be grown as a hedge.

Size H and S: 4–5 ft. **Aspect** Prefers full sun, but tolerates light shade. **Hardiness** Hardy. **Soil** Any well-drained garden soil. **After-care** From two years after planting, remove one-third of the old flowering wood annually after flowering; this will encourage rejuvenation from the base and the production of good flowering wood. When grown as a hedge, prune regularly. **Planting partners** *Berberis thunbergii* 'Halmond's Pillar,' *Sedum* 'Herbstfreude,' *Artemisia absinthium* 'Lambrook Silver.'

Winter-flowering currant see
Ribes laurifolium

Yew see *Taxus baccata*

Weigela florida 'Variegata'

Intermediate plants

Bamboo see **Pleioblastus auricomus**

Broom see *Cytisus* 'Lena'

Ceanothus 'Blue Mound'

This low, hummock-forming shrub, with its bright foliage, provides an effective backdrop for displays of smaller edging perennials. In early summer, showers of deep blue flower panicles cover its glossy evergreen foliage, making a dramatic display. The taller-growing *C. impressus* and *C.* 'Puget Blue' form excellent fan-trained wall shrubs in a small, sheltered garden.
Size H: 2–3 ft.; S: 3 ft. 3 in.–4 ft. **Aspect** Full sun. **Hardiness** Moderately hardy. **Soil** Any well drained garden soil, acid to slightly alkaline. **After-care** If damaged in a severe winter, cut back to non-damaged wood so that new growth regenerates from below, or just above soil level. **Planting partners** *Potentilla fruticosa* 'Knap Hill,' *Campanula glomerata* 'Superba,' *Scilla siberica*.

Cistus

Many within this group of evergreen shrubs with a rounded habit grow to only about 3 ft., so are suitable in a confined space. They thrive in a hot, dry part of the garden and are freely flowering from early to late summer. *C. × corbariensis* has dark, sage-green leaves which complement gray foliage; the single white flowers open daily from crimson-tinted buds. *C.* 'Silver Pink' has gray-green leaves with silver-pink flowers and yellow stamens. *C.* 'Sunset' has deep cerise-pink flowers set above gray foliage and associates particularly well with soft pink flowers.
Size H: 2–2½ ft.; S: 2½–3 ft. **Aspect** Full sun. **Hardiness** Moderately hardy. **Soil** Most well-drained garden soils. **After-care** Trim back lightly each year to increase flowering. **Planting partners** with *C. × corbariensis*: *Santolina* 'Lemon Queen,' *Perovskia* 'Blue Spire'; with *C.* 'Silver Pink': *Heuchera* 'Palace Purple,' *Santolina chamaecyparissus*; with *C.* 'Sunset': *Lavatera* 'Pink Frills,' *Lavandula angustifolia* 'Hidcote.'

Cytisus 'Lena'
Broom

This is my favorite of the spring and early summer-flowering brooms for a small garden, due to its compact habit of growth. The startling hot shades of the bicolor ruby-red and yellow pea-shaped blooms will draw the eye and set any sunny corner alight for a few weeks. The green wispy branches and insignificant leaves will blend into adjacent planting throughout the rest of the year.
Size H and S: 2–3 ft. **Aspect** Full sun. **Hardiness** Hardy. **Soil** Well drained, neutral to acid soil but will tolerate some alkalinity. **After-care** Remove half the current season's growth after flowering. Relatively short lived: replace after 10 years. **Planting partners** *Juniperus × media* 'Old Gold,' *Taxus baccata* 'Fastigiata,' *Euphorbia characias wulfenii*.

Ceanothus 'Blue Mound'

The middle layer of planting includes smaller-growing shrubs for additional structure as well as perennials to provide bold splashes of flower color.

Daphne odora
'Aureomarginata'
Winter daphne

An evergreen shrub, its purple-pink, trumpet-shaped flowers are delicately fragrant in late winter/early spring. Its broad leaves are gold-edged.
Size H: 2 ft. 9 in.–3 ft.; S: 3 ft. 3 in. **Aspect** Prefers light shade. **Hardiness** Moderately hardy. **Soil** Prefers a rich, deep loam. **After-care** No pruning required; can become lax and woody, but rejuvenation by pruning is rarely successful. **Planting partners** *Helleborus niger*, *Erica carnea* 'Pink Spangles,' *Hosta* 'Gold Standard.'

Hebe rakaiensis

This species offers structural form in plant groupings. The perfectly symmetrical, dome-shaped shrub makes an ideal accent point or full stop, for example at the end of a planting group or path. It has dainty, bright green ovate foliage all year round and intermittent racemes of delicate white flowers through spring and summer. Smaller hebes with a carpeting habit or more prominent flowers are included as decorative infill (see pages 121–2). **Size** H: 1½ ft.; S: 3 ft. 3 in. **Aspect** Prefers full sun, but tolerates light shade. **Hardiness** Moderately hardy. **Soil** Any well-drained, open garden soil. **After-care** Trim over annually in early spring. May be cut back hard, almost to ground level, every 3–4 years to induce strong, healthy new shoots. **Planting partners** Short-growing spring bulbs, *Saxifraga × urbium* 'Variegata,' *Anaphalis triplinervis* 'Summer Snow,' *Iris foetidissima* 'Variegata,' *Festuca glauca* 'Blauglut.'

Juniperus
Juniper

The prostrate-growing forms of this conifer offer year-round foliage color and an interesting habit of growth ideal for a small garden, especially to drape over the wall of a raised bed. *J. × media* 'Old Gold' has ascending branches which droop at the tips, is of compact habit and retains its bronze-gold foliage throughout the winter; size H: 3 ft. 3 in.; S: 4 ft. *J. horizontalis* 'Wiltonii' is one of the flattest carpet junipers, with glaucous to silver-blue foliage; size H: 2–4 in.; S: 6½–10 ft. *J. conferta* has prickly apple-green foliage and is prostrate with shortly ascending branches; size H: 4–8 in.; S: 6½–13 ft.
Size H and S: As above. **Aspect** Sun. **Hardiness** Hardy. **Soil** Any garden soil; this is the most suitable conifer for alkaline soils. **After-care** Some prostrate or semi-prostrate junipers may become overgrown and unshapely, in which case prune back to make a more compact plant. Apply a dressing of general fertilizer annually in spring. **Planting partners** with gold-foliaged cultivars: *Santolina chamaecyparissus, Crocosmia* 'Emily McKenzie'; with green-leaved cultivars: evergreen azalea; with blue-leaved cultivars: *Salvia officinalis* 'Purparescens,' *Diascia vigilis.*

Lavandula
Lavender

The lavender scent of both flowers and foliage add a touch of the Mediterranean to any small sunny corner. These aromatic small shrubs will form low hedging or edging plants that associate well with a wide range of shrubs and perennials, especially in the pink, blue and clear yellow range, *L. angustifolia* 'Hidcote' forms a compact bush of gray-green foliage with a profusion of dense violet-blue flower spikes in mid-summer. *L. angustifolia* 'Nana Alba' is equally tidy and bears almost white flower spikes over slightly more silver foliage; 'Rosea' displays blue-pink flowers and is a good coastal plant. *L. stoechas pedunculata* (French lavender) has dense terminal heads of scented, dark purple flowerheads from which a few narrow wispy lilac-blue bracts emerge, a most attractive subspecies.
Size H: 12–20 in.; S: 20 in.–2½ ft. **Aspect** Full sun. **Hardiness** Moderately hardy. **Soil** Well drained and light. **After-care** Trim back with shears after flowering and lightly shape in spring. **Planting partners** *Diascia rigescens, Verbena* 'Silver Anne,' *Stachys byzantina* 'Silver Carpet,' *Santolina chamaecyparissus* 'Nana.'

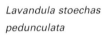

Lavandula stoechas pedunculata

Lavatera 'Pink Frills'
Tree mallow

A vigorous growing shrub, worth including in the small garden for its long flowering season. The continuous display of pale pink, cup-shaped blooms with prettily frilled petals and a deeper wine-red center adorn the gray-green foliage from midsummer to mid-autumn.

Size H: 4–5 ft.; S: 3 ft. 3 in.–4 ft. **Aspect** Full sun. **Hardiness** Moderately hard: minimum winter temperature 23°F, below which plants may be killed. **Soil** Any well-drained garden soil. **After-care** All the previous year's shoots should be cut hard back annually in early spring to encourage flowering. **Planting partners** *Tamarix ramosissima*, *Olearia × haastii*, *Berberis thunbergii atropurpurea*.

Lavender see *Lavandula*

Lonicera nitida
'Baggesen's Gold'

The dainty, bright gold, glossy leaves of this shrub are particularly effective in winter and spring when the foliage appears most golden. They contrast well with bold leaf shapes and deep blue and lilac flowers. *Lonicera nitida* can be used as a hedge since it responds well to clipping. When well fed, it also grows happily in a container. Can be cut for flower arranging.

Size H: 4 ft.; S: 5 ft., if unclipped. **Aspect** Sun for best leaf color, though it will grow in semi-shade. **Hardiness** Hardy. **Soil** Any garden soil that is

neither extremely dry nor waterlogged. **After-care** Trim regularly to retain desired shape and size. Remove one-third of old wood each spring to rejuvenate. It may be cut down to ground level and will regrow. **Planting partners** *Salvia officinalis* 'Purpurascens,' *Euonymus fortunei* 'Emerald 'n Gold,' *Campanula glomerata* 'Superba.'

Pleioblastus auricomus
Bamboo

The rich yellow striped foliage held on erect purplish-green canes will brighten any dull corner, particularly in winter. This is the best variegated bamboo for the small garden and for pots, tending to be smaller in less favorable conditions.

Size H: up to 4 ft.; S: Spreads slowly. **Aspect** Light to deep shade. **Hardiness** Hardy. **Soil** Any garden soil. **After-care** Old canes may be cut to ground level in autumn to encourage new growth. **Planting partners** *Aster amellus* 'Violet Queen,' *Alchemilla mollis*, *Berberis thunbergii atropurpurea*.

Rhododendron
Azalea, dwarf evergreen species

In a protected small garden with acid soil, the glossy, dark green foliage of this group of evergreen shrubs provides invaluable mid-height structure for any planting group. Of Japanese origin and found naturally in woodland glades, azaleas make ideal subjects for partial shade and, when grouped, create an enchanting patch-

Lavatera 'Pink Frills'

work of color in spring. Their slow, compact habit of growth means they entail very little maintenance. A small selection from the many available include: 'Blaauw's Pink,' salmon pink with paler shading, early-flowering; 'Palestrina,' pure white with a faint hint of green; 'Vuyk's Scarlet,' bright red with wavy petals; 'Orange Beauty,' salmon-orange.

Size H: 2 ft.–3 ft. 3 in.; S: 2–4 ft. **Aspect** Partial shade; will tolerate full sun if the roots are protected. **Hardiness** Hardy, though cold winds in winter may cause defoliation if there is no protection. **Soil** Acid, preferably rich in leaf mold. **After-care** Remove damaged wood. **Planting partners** *Garrya elliptica*, ferns, *Pulmonaria officinalis* 'Sissinghurst White.'

Sage see *Salvia officinalis*

Salvia officinalis
Sage

This aromatic shrub is a valuable asset to small-garden plant groupings. The new growth of the rough-textured leaves looks at its best in spring and summer and is particularly effective in colored foliage groups. The two-

Salvia officinalis 'Purpurascens'

lipped blue flowers are borne in whorls along the stems in summer, adding to the pleasing effect. 'Purpurascens' has attractive leaves, washed over with purple; 'Tricolor' has even brighter purple foliage, mottled with pink and white; 'Icterina' has golden variegated foliage and mixes well in a gold and blue color scheme.

Size H: 2–2½ ft.; S: 2½–3 ft. 3 in. **Aspect** Full sun; will also grow in very light shade; but foliage color will be less good. **Hardiness** Moderately hardy; may be damaged in a very severe winter. **Soil** Warm and well drained. **After-care** In spring, reduce last season's growth by half, to keep the shrub young and healthy; replace plants every 3–5 years. **Planting partners** *Carex oshimensis* 'Evergold,' *Alchemilla mollis*, *Fragaria × ananassa* 'Variegata,' *Rosa* 'Hermosa.'

Skimmia japonica
'Rubella'

A useful compact shrub, tolerant of coastal winds, shade and industrial pollution. It has large, ovate to elliptical, leathery dark green leaves and purple veins and a silver underside. A male clone with large panicles of open, red buds throughout the winter looks attractive in pots. Use this as a pollinator for the female, *S. japonica* 'Veitchii,' which is strong-growing and bears clusters of brilliant red fruits in late summer/autumn. If there is room for only one plant, grow the hermaphrodite *S. reevesiana*, forming a low, compact mound rarely reaching more than 3 ft.; it produces white panicles

of flowers in early summer; these are followed by egg-shaped, matt crimson-red fruit which appear later in the season.

Size H and S: 3 ft.–3 ft. 3 in. **Aspect** Ideal for medium shade, but tolerates full sun. **Hardiness** Hardy. **Soil** Deep acid soil. **After-care** No pruning required. Branches may be cut back and will rejuvenate from the base. **Planting partners** *Persicaria affinis* 'Superba,' *Cornus sanguinea* 'Winter Flame.'

Viburnum davidii

The beautiful shape of this shrub and the texture of its bold, leathery evergreen leaves makes it a worthwhile inclusion in a group of plants, lending substance throughout the year. Flat clusters of white flowers open from deep pink buds in early summer and bright turquoise berries follow on female plants if there is a nearby male for pollination. It makes a good partner with small-leaved shrubs and perennials.

Size H: 2½ ft.–3 ft. 3 in.; S: 2–2½ ft. **Aspect** Prefers light shade. **Hardiness** Hardy. **Soil** Prefers a rich soil, not waterlogged. **After-care** It can be reduced in size by pruning if wished. **Planting partners** *Buxus sempervirens*, *Soleirolia soleirolii*, *Coreopsis verticillata* 'Moonbeam.'

Tree mallow see
Lavatera 'Pink Frills'
Winter daphne see *Daphne odora*
'Aureomarginata'

Decorative infill

Alchemilla ellenbeckii

This very dainty lady's mantle is ideal for growing in gravel or paving. It has finely divided foliage on bright red stems with tiny sprays of lime-green stars in midsummer.

Size H: 4 in.; S: 12 in. **Aspect** Full sun to very light shade. **Hardiness** Hardy. **Soil** Any garden soil. **After-care** Feed with general fertilizer in early to mid-spring and again after removing the fading flower spikes in midsummer. **Planting partners** *Euphorbia characias wulfenii* 'Humpty Dumpty,' *Artemisia stelleriana*.

Campanula portenschlagiana

Above the dense cover of heart-shaped, mid-green leaves, a mass of deep blue-purple bell-shaped flowers appear from midsummer to autumn. An ideal perennial for planting in front of large shrubs, in narrow spaces or gaps in paving, this species spreads easily.

Size H: 6 in.; S: 1½–2 ft. **Aspect** Full sun to medium shade. **Hardiness** Hardy. **Soil** Flourishes in a well-drained fertile soil; tolerates dry areas. **After-care** Weed out unwanted seedlings. Feed with general fertilizer in early spring and remove faded flower spikes in summer. **Planting partners** *Cytisus battandieri*, *Geranium sanguineum* 'Lancastriense.'

Christmas box see
Sarcococca bookeriana var. *digyna*

Coral bells see *Heuchera micrantha* 'Palace Purple'

Dianthus
Pink

The long flowering season of the perpetual pinks makes them good-value edging plants in a limited space. The silver-gray tufted mats of evergreen foliage set off the range of pink and white flowers during the summer. Pale pink blooms with a darker plum detail will pick out the purple shades of foliage plants nearby. Select cultivars with scented flowers such as 'Doris,' shrimp-pink with a red eye, 'White Ladies,' double white ragged petals, or 'Diane,' with deeper salmon-red double blooms.

Size H and S: 12 in. **Aspect** Full sun. **Hardiness** Hardy. **Soil** Well drained; pinks prefer alkaline soil, so add garden lime periodically. **After-care** Feed with general fertilizer in mid-spring and a high-potash fertilizer after flowering. Dead-head regularly. Replace every three to five years. **Planting partners** *Iris pallida* 'Variegata,' *Thymus × citriodorus* 'Variegatus,' *Salvia officinalis* 'Purpurascens.'

Erica carnea
Heather

These winter-flowering heathers, which tolerate both lime and some shade, are useful ground-covering plants, suffering little damage in hard winters. 'Pink Spangles' has masses of pink bells from mid-winter to spring, set against bright green healthy foliage. The dark green foliage of 'Myretoun Ruby' is a useful foil for pink summer-flowering perennials such as *Diascia* and *Saponaria* and in late winter/early spring it is covered with a carpet of

Dianthus 'Doris'

Whether tucked among taller shrubs, edging a path, climbing over an arch or sitting at the front of a border, these plants play an eye-catching role in the overall display.

large, glowing rich pink to ruby-red bells. 'Foxhollow' has bright golden summer foliage, tinged pink and red in winter, with a few lavender flowers; 'Ann Sparkes' has orange-yellow foliage tipped bronze-red, with purple flowers in late winter.

Size H: 6 in.; S: 8–16 in. **Aspect** Sunny and open but will tolerate partial shade. **Hardiness** Hardy. **Soil** Prefers acid soil but will tolerate and grow in an alkaline soil. **After-care** Trim lightly after flowering to induce new growth. **Planting partners** *Helleborus foetidus*, *Euonymus fortunei*, low-growing junipers, spring-flowering viburnums.

Euonymus fortunei
'Silver Queen'

Euonymus fortunei

An invaluable evergreen foliage shrub offering good texture and dense enough to provide winter structure in the small garden. The small, ovate leaves range from green to silver- and gold-variegated, acting as a good foil to adjacent seasonal flowers. They may be planted as ground cover or trained on a wall. 'Emerald Gaiety' has gray-green leaves, margined white; 'Emerald 'n Gold' has gray-green leaves with gold margins; 'Silver Queen' has larger, creamy yellow leaves in spring, fading to green with creamy margins.

Size H and S: 2–3 ft. **Aspect** Sun or shade. **Hardiness** Hardy; may lose some leaves in extreme cold. **Soil** Any garden soil. **After-care** No regular pruning required but may be clipped. **Planting partners** with silver variegation: *Choisya ternata*, *Artemisia absinthium* 'Lambrook Silver'; with gold variegation: *Helleborus foetidus*, *Humulus lupulus* 'Aureus.'

Gardener's garters see *Phalaris arundinacea picta* 'Feesey'

Ferns

A damp, shady corner, sheltered from strong winds, is an ideal site for ferns and other shade-loving plants. The delicate, finely divided soft green fronds of *Polystichum setiferum* (Percristatum group) are retained throughout winter as are the bright green, leathery spear-shaped fronds of *Asplenium scolopendrium* (hart's tongue fern), arising from a central crown; both grow 2½ ft. tall and spread up to 3 ft. 3 in. *Blechnum penna-marina alpinum* makes excellent evergreen ground cover in shade, spreading by creeping rhizomes which produce small ladder-shaped fronds 12 in. high and wide.

Size H and S: see above. **Aspect** Shade. **Hardiness** Hardy. **Soil** Any moist soil that is rich in organic matter. **After-care** Mulch with leaf mold in autumn for winter protection; keep moist in summer. Remove dead or untidy leaves in spring. **Planting partners** *Hosta*, *Tiarella cordifolia*, *Soldanella villosa*, *Bergenia*.

Hebe

The low-growing evergreen forms of *Hebe*, with their tidy habit of growth throughout the year, make excellent framework shrubs. Flowerheads in shades of pink, white or lilac adorn the bush from spring to early autumn. Being resistant to pollution and salt spray, they are especially useful. Equally happy in pots, *H. albicans* and *H. pinguifolia* 'Pagei' have silver-gray foliage which sets off the pale pink or dark blue and violet flowers. *Hebe albicans* 'Red Edge,' with a delicate wine-red line around the leaf margin, associates well with cerise flowers and foliage; *H.* 'Autumn Glory' produces deep purple-blue racemes of flowers above its dark, purple-green, rounded foliage; newer cultivars are the pink-flowered *H.* 'Rosie' and pale lilac-flowered *H.* 'Marjorie.'

Size H: 12–18 in.; S: 3 ft. 3 in. **Aspect** Full sun, but tolerates light shade. **Hardiness** Moderately hardy; may be damaged in very cold winters but generally survive. **Soil** Any well-drained garden soil. **After-care** Trim over lightly each spring to encourage new growth. **Planting partners** *Rosa* 'The Fairy,' *Salvia officinalis* 'Purpurascens,' *Phlox*.

Heuchera micrantha
'Palace Purple'
Coral bells

This perennial has striking heart-shaped, bronze-red leaves which are light magenta-pink on the undersides. This year-round foliage is transformed in summer by wiry stems bearing tiny feathery white flowers which turn into small rosy-bronze seed heads in late summer/autumn. *Heuchera* 'Snowstorm,' with scallop-shaped leaves that are almost entirely cream in summer, and with bright red flower spikes, is equally appealing as a filler for the front of the display; if well fed, it makes an unusual specimen in a pot.

Size H and S: 1½–2 ft. **Aspect** Full sun to part-shade. **Hardiness** Hardy. **Soil** Any garden soil. **After-care** Apply a general fertilizer in mid-spring. Leave the foliage to give winter interest then tidy and mulch in spring.

Planting partners *Festuca glauca*, *Cistus* 'Silver Pink,' *Hemerocallis* 'Catherine Woodbury.'

Horned violet see *Viola cornuta*

Phalaris arundinacea picta 'Feesey'
Gardener's garters

A superior, less invasive form of the more commonly seen ribbon grass, with brilliant white-striped strap-shaped leaves and a compact habit of growth. It associates well with white-variegated or purple foliage plants. It looks appropriate adjacent to water. **Size** H and S: 2 ft. **Aspect** Sun or part-shade. **Hardiness** Hardy. **Soil** Any garden soil. **After-care** Divide every few years to rejuvenate. **Planting partners** *Weigela praecox* 'Variegata,' *Salvia officinalis* 'Purpurascens,' *Phlox paniculata* 'Blue Ice.'

Pink see *Dianthus*

Sarcococca hookeriana var. *digyna*
Christmas box

There is often an awkward shady corner adjacent to a house wall or alongside a path where this non-invasive yet suckering evergreen shrub will provide welcome foliage with its glossy, small, slender leaves. In winter, insignificant but fragrant white flowers appear, followed by black berries.
Size H: 2–3 ft.; S: 16 in. **Aspect** Full

sun to medium shade. **Hardiness** Very hardy. **Soil** Any well-fed garden soil. **After-care** No pruning needed; mulch with leaf-mold compost. **Planting partners** *Helleborus orientalis*, *Narcissus* 'February Gold,' *Santolina chamaecyparissus*, ferns.

Saxifraga 'Rubrifolia'

This is a choice plant for a special corner of the garden. Glistening white, star-shaped flowers appear on rose-pink stems in late autumn/early winter above the bronze-red shiny leaves, which look almost succulent. **Size** H: 12–15 in.; S: 1–1½ ft. **Aspect** Cool, half shade. **Hardiness** Moderately hardy. **Soil** Rich and moist. **After-care** Remove faded flower spikes. **Planting partners** *Ajuga reptans* 'Pink Elf,' *Dryopteris filix-mas*, and *Photinia × fraseri* 'Birmingham.'

Spiked speedwell
see *Veronica austriaca teucrium*
'Crater Lake Blue'

Veronica austriaca teucrium 'Crater Lake Blue'
Spiked speedwell

This easy, low-growing perennial produces deep gentian-blue flower spikes from mid- to late summer. The semi-evergreen foliage is bright and shiny; it looks most effective massed as a clump along a path or border edge. It associates well with water.
Size H: 12 in.; S: 1½–2 ft. **Aspect** Full sun to light shade. **Hardiness**

Hebe 'Fall Glory'

Hardy. **Soil** Any garden soil. **After-care** Cut to ground level in autumn; feed with general fertilizer in spring. **Planting partners** *Santolina chamaecyparissus* 'Nana,' *Choisya ternata* 'Sundance.'

Viola cornuta
Horned violet

This delightful little perennial will freely spread and provide a carpet of blue flowers from spring to autumn; the white form, *V. cornuta* 'Alba,' flowers almost as freely. *V.* 'Clementina' displays vivid violet-blue flowers which glisten when adjacent to gold foliage.
Size H: 6–8 in.; S: 12 in. **Aspect** Sun or part-shade. **Hardiness** Hardy. **Soil** Any garden soil, preferably enriched with humus. **After-care** Feed with general fertilizer in early spring and again in midsummer. Trim lightly after flowering to maintain a good shape and encourage perpetual flowering. **Planting partners** A wide range of perennials, shrubs and conifers.

Index

Page numbers in *italics* refer to illustrations; numbers in **bold** to the chapter "Key Plants."

Abutilon 80
Acacia dealbata 75 (9–11)
Acaena 83
Acanthus 7, 19, 38
Accent planting 72–3
Acer see Maple
Achillea 79
  A. 'Moonshine' 41 (3–8)
  Acid soil 17
Acorus calamus 60 (4–9)
Actinidia kolomikta 50, 75, *80*, *106* (4–8)
Adiantum pedatum 81 (3–8)
Agapanthus 77
  A. campanulatus 69 (8–11)
  A. campanulatus albidus 68 (8–11)
Ajuga reptans 18, 40, 105 (3–8)
Alchemilla
  A. ellenbeckii 121 (4–7)
  A. erythropoda 60 (3–7)
  A. mollis 18, *67*, *69*, 106, *109* (4–7)
Alkaline soil 17
Allium afflatunense 52 (4–8)
Alnus incana 71 (3–6)
Aloysia see Lemon verbena
Amelanchier 106
  A. canadensis see Snowy mespilus
  A. lamarckii 70 (3–8)
Anaphalis triplinervis 118 (3–8)
Anchusa 67
Anemone blanda 84 (5–8)
Anemone hupehensis 110 (4–8)
Anemone × hybrida 68 (5–8)
Anthemis punctata cupaniana 41, 77 (5–9)
Anthriscus sylvestris 85 (5–9)
Aponogeton distachyos 60 (9–11)
Apple (*Malus*) 55, 71, **110–11** (4–8)
Aquatic plants 60
Arabis alpina 69 (4–7)
Arbors 19, 58, 75
Arches *11*, 34, 54, 58, 59
Argyranthemum see Marguerites
Artemisia 78, *84*
  A. absinthium 116 (5–8)
  A. 'Powis Castle' 41 (5–8)
Arum italicum 60 (6–9)
Arum lily *8*
Arundinaria see Bamboo
Ash (*Fraxinus*) 19
Asperula odorata 76 (4–8)
Asplenium see Hart's tongue fern
Aster 76, 107
  A. amellus 119 (4–8)
  A. × frikartii 85 (5–8)
  A. novae-angliae 78 (5–8)

Astilbe 17
Astrantia major 79 (4–7)
Athyrium niponicum pictum 76 (3–9)
Aubrieta 59
Aucuba japonica 18, *85* (7–9)
Autumn
  tasks 106–7
Autumn-flowering cherry (*Prunus*) 71, 78, **111**
Azaleas 17, 38, **119**
Azolla caroliniana 60 (7–11)

Background planting 72, 74–5
Balance 28
Balconies 19, 53, 82
Bamboo 18, *27*, 38, *39*
  Fargesia murieliae 65 (4–9)
  Pleioblastus auricomus 57, *85*, **119** (5–9)
Barbecues *33*
Bark chippings 46, 89
Bay (*Laurus*) 38, 96
  L. nobilis 57, 59, 83 (8–10)
Beech (*Fagus*) 55
Benches *see* Furniture
Berberis 34, 54
  B. darwinii 74 (7–9)
  B. × stenophylla 55 (6–9)
  B. thunbergii 35, 40, 54, *76*, 106 (5–8)
Bergenia 18, *35*, 76, 77, 104
  B. 'Abendglut' *35*, 76 (4–8)
  B. stracheyi 68 (4–8)
Berries 75, 107, 115
Betula see Birch
Birch (*Betula*)
  B. jacquemontii *33* (5–7)
  B. pendula 19, *33*, 71 (3–6)
Billardiera longiflora 80 (7–9)
Blechnum
  see also Ferns
  B. penna-marina 76 (6–9)
  B. penna-marina alpinum 122 (6–9)
Box (*Buxus*) *21*, *27*, *37*, *39*, 55
  accent plant *73*
  B. sempervirens 38, 55, 59, 68 (6–8)
Boundaries 49–55
  planning 14, 26
  plants 75
Brachyglottis 41, 74, 79 (9–10)
Brick 26, 42–3, 50
Broom (*Cytisus*) 96, 98, **117**
  C. battandieri 83 (8–9)
  C. 'Lena' **117** (7–9)
Buckthorn (*Rhamnus*) 115
Buddleia davidii 74, 95, 96 (5–9)
Budget 9, 24–5
Bulbs 77, 82, 83
Busy lizzy (*Impatiens*) 82
Buxus see Box

Calamondin orange 82 (9–11)
Caltha palustris 60 (3–9)
Camellia 38, 57, 76, 104

conditions required 17, 19, 75
  C. 'Cornish Snow' 76 (7–9)
  C. japonica 79 (7–9)
  C. × williamsii 75 (7–9)
Campanula 76, 106
  C. garganica 83 (4–8)
  C. glomerata **117** (5–8)
  C. lactiflora 68 (4–8)
  C. latiloba 73 (4–8)
  C. portenschlagiana 22, *33*, **121** (4–8)
Car space 23
Caragana arborescens 73 (2–7)
Carex
  C. morrowii 77 (5–9)
  C. oshimensis **120** (5–8)
Cattail *82*
Ceanothus 74, 79, *79*, **117**
  conditions required 17, 19, 75
  pruning 95, 96
  wall-training 98
  C. 'Blue Mound' 79, **117** (8–10)
  C. 'Concha' *79* (8–10)
  C. 'Delight' 74 (8–10)
  C. × delileanus 74 (7–10)
  C. impressus 74 (8–10)
Ceratostigma plumbaginoides 78, 85 (5–8)
Chaenomeles 38, 96, 98
  C. speciosa 54, 77 (5–8)
  C. × superba 75, *81* (5–9)
Chamaecyparis lawsoniana see Lawson cypress

Chamomile (*Chamaemelum*) lawn 47
  C. nobile 83 (6–9)
Cherry laurel (*Prunus laurocerasus*) 18, 19, 74, **114**
  pruning 69, 95, 96 (7–9)
Cherry (*Prunus*) *17*, 38, 55, 70, 71
  P. × subhirtella 71, 78, **111** (6–8)
Choisya see Mexican orange blossom
Christmas box (*Sarcococca*)
  S. hookeriana var. *digyna* **123** (6–8)
  S. humilis 76, 82, 83, 104 (6–8)
Cimicifuga simplex 41 (3–8)
Cistus 38, 76, 104, 106, **117**
  pruning 95, 96
  C. × corbariensis 76 (7–9)
  C. × pulverulentus 80 (7–9)
  C. 'Silver Pink' **117** (7–9)
  C. 'Sunset' 76, **117** (7–9)
× *Citrofortunella microcarpa* 82 (9–11)
Classical gardens 10–11
Clay pavers 42–3
Clay soil 16
Clematis 35, *76*, *78*, *80*, *106*, **112**
  containers 57
  frost damage 104
  pillars 59

pruning 96–7
shade-tolerant 75
  C. 'Alice Fisk' **112** (4–8)
  C. alpina 75, *81*, *84*, **114** (4–9)
  C. armandii 58, 77, *80* (7–9)
  C. 'Asao' **112** (4–8)
  C. 'Barbara Jackman' **112** (4–8)
  C. 'Bees' Jubilee' 35 (4–8)
  C. 'Beauty of Worcester' 57 (4–8)
  C. cirrhosa balearica 77, *112*, *113* (7–9)
  C. 'Comtesse de Bouchaud' 75 (4–8)
  C. 'Dawn' 57, **112** (4–8)
  C. 'Doctor Ruppel' **112** (4–8)
  C. 'Edith' **112** (4–8)
  C. florida 50 (6–9)
  C. 'Hagley Hybrid' 57, **112** (4–8)
  C. Haku-ookan' 57 (4–8)
  C. 'H. F. Young' 57 (4–8)
  C. jackmanii 99 (4–9)
  C. 'Lasurstern' 75 (4–8)
  C. macropetala **113** (6–9)
  C. 'Marie Boisselot' 75 (4–8)
  C. 'Minuet' **113** (4–8)
  C. montana 52, 54, 58, 59 (6–9)
  C. 'Nelly Moser' *51*, 75 (4–8)
  C. 'Rouge Cardinal' **112** (4–8)
  C. tangutica 41 (3–8)
  C. 'The President' **112** (4–8)

Plant hardiness zones

This hardiness map will help you to establish which plants are most suitable for your garden. **The zones 1–11 are based on the average annual minimum temperature for each zone and appear after the plant entry in the index.** The lower number indicates the northernmost zone in which the plant can survive the winter and the higher number the most southerly area in which it will perform consistently.

ZONE 1	BELOW −50° F
ZONE 2	−50° TO −40°
ZONE 3	−40° TO −30°
ZONE 4	−30° TO −20°
ZONE 5	−20° TO −10°
ZONE 6	−10° TO 0°
ZONE 7	0° TO 10°
ZONE 8	10° TO 20°
ZONE 9	20° TO 30°
ZONE 10	30° TO 40°
ZONE 11	ABOVE 40°

Acknowledgments

The publishers wish to thank the following photographers and organizations for their kind permission to reproduce the photographs in this book:

1 Gary Rogers; 2–3 Jerry Harpur (designer: Jane Alexander-Sinclair); 4–7 Brigitte Thomas; 8 John Glover; 9 Jerry Harpur (designer: Arabella Lennox-Boyd); 10 Gary Moyes; 11 above Georges Lévêque (designer: J. Wirtz, Belgium); 11 below Hugh Palmer; 12–13 Jerry Harpur (designer: Judith Sharpe); 14 Brigitte Thomas; 15 Jerry Harpur (designer: Penny Crawshaw); 17 Jerry Harpur (designer: Gunilla Pickard); 19 Jerry Harpur (designer: Keith Corlett); 21 Jerry Harpur (designer: Christopher Masson); 22 Jerry Harpur (designer: Julie Toll, London); 23 Jerry Harpur (Michael Balston Design); 25 John Fielding; 26 Jerry Harpur (designer: Christopher Masson); 27 Brigitte Thomas; 28 Noel Kavanagh (designer: Julie Toll); 36–7 Jerry Harpur (designer: Christopher Masson); 38 Karl Dietrich-Bühler/ Elizabeth Whiting and Associates; 39 Noel Kavanagh (designer: Richard Baxter); 40 Christopher Simon-Sykes/The Interior World; 41 Jerry Harpur (Edwina von Gal, N.Y.); 42 Jerry Harpur (designer: Judith Sharpe); 43 above Jerry Harpur (designer: Julie Toll); 43 below Jerry Harpur; 44 above Denise Clyne/Garden Picture Library; 44 below Christopher Simon-Sykes/Camera Press; 45 Eric Crichton (Mrs. Sinclair, Lime Tree Cottage, Surrey); 46 Jerry Harpur (designer: Simon Frazer); 47 Georges Lévêque (designer: Ed. Avadeen); 49 John Heseltine; 50 Brigitte Thomas; 51 Michèle Lamontagne; 52 Andrew Lawson (Gothic House, Oxfordshire); 53 Brigitte Thomas; 55 Eric Crichton; 56 Jerry Harpur (designer: Perry Guillot); 57 John Glover (Toad Cottage, Berkshire); 58 Noel Kavanagh (designer: Richard Baxter); 59 Andrew Lawson (designer: Simon Driver); 61 Jerry Harpur (designer: Christopher Masson); 63 Jerry Harpur (Rod Taylor, Hank Litho, The Cape, South Africa); 64–5 Clive Nichols (Turn End, Buckinghamshire); 67 Jerry Harpur (designer: Arabella Lennox-Boyd); 68 Neil Campbell-Sharp (Bosvigo House, Cornwall); 69 above Jerry Harpur (Rofford Manor, Oxfordshire); 69 below Brigitte Thomas; 71 John Glover (The Anchorage, Kent); 72 John Fielding; 73 John Glover (Tomasina Beck, London); 74 Jerry Harpur/Elizabeth Whiting and Associates; 75 Jerry Harpur; 76 John Glover (22 Beechcroft Road, Oxford); 77 John Glover; 78 John Glover (The Anchorage, Kent); 79 Brigitte Thomas; 82 Jerry Harpur (designer: Phillip Watson); 83 Jerry Harpur/ Elizabeth Whiting and Associates; 86–7 Beatrice Pichon (Le Jardin d'Anne-Marie); 89 Jerry Harpur (designer: Pamela Stewart); 90 Howard Rice/Garden Picture Library; 92 Noel Kavanagh (designer: Julie Toll); 93 John Glover (Hillgrove Crescent, Kiddeminster); 95 Brigitte Thomas; 99 Christian Sarramon; 102–5 S and O Mathews; 106–7 John Glover; 108–9 Georges Lévêque; 110 John Glover (a private garden, Staffordshire); 112 John Glover (Burford House, Shropshire); 114–15 Neil Campbell-Sharp; 116 Eric Crichton; 118 John Fielding; 119 Christopher Fairweather/Garden Picture Library; 120 John Glover; 122 Eric Crichton (Barnsley House); 123 Neil Holmes.

The publishers also thank Helen Ridge, Barbara Nash and Janet Smy.
Index compiled by Indexing Specialists, Hove, East Sussex BN3 2DJ.